INNER FIRE

INNER FIRE

YOUR WILL TO LIVE

Stories of Courage, Hope, and Determination

Ernest H. Rosenbaum, M.D. and Isadora R. Rosenbaum, M.A.

with Mark Mandel, Greg Cable, Tina Anderson, and Gail Gordon

Introduction by David Spiegel, M.D.

Plexus

815-A Brazos, Suite 445-Y

Austin, Texas 78701

Design and Typography: Michael Diehl

Cover Image: Ed Freeman

9 8 7 6 5 4 3 2 1

First Edition

Printed in the United States on acid free paper

Library of Congress Catalog Card Number: 98-86771

The will to live is in both

your heart and your mind.

To those who have dedicated their lives to relieving
human suffering, including the dedicated, skilled,
and highly proficient physicians, nurses, and staff
at the UCSF/Mount Zion Hospital Intensive Care Unit,
who saved my life in the summer of 1995.

And to the contributors to this book,
who exemplify the "Will To Live."

CONTENTS

Pseudonyms have been used to protect the privacy of some contributors

ACKNOWLEDGMENTS

WE WISH TO GIVE SPECIAL THANKS AND RECOGNITION to our editors: Faye Volk; Paul Volk; Mary Heldman; Laura Rosenbaum; Lillian Snyder; Glenda Derman; Chana Lotan, M.D.; Susan Claymon; Jackie Lowenberg; Sabrina Selim; and Stephanie Holt; for their thoughtful reviews which helped shape the concepts in this book to make it clear, concise, and more understandable.

We wish to thank Paula Chung, Diane McElhiney, and Michael Glover for their tireless efforts, support, and creative talents that helped to produce this book.

PREFACE

MEDICAL ONCOLOGISTS have always been fascinated by the power of the will to live. What makes a person faced with a life-threatening crisis fight to live? How do people cope with chronic disease or refuse to let physical discomfort keep them from enjoying their family, friends, and outside interests? We feel that the answer to questions such as these has to do with the will to live.

In trying to find how certain people were able to overcome such obstacles, we began asking them about their will to live. What promoted their ability to cope under the stress of disease and get so much out of life, no matter what the circumstances?

We discovered a commonality of factors among both those who live with acute and chronic disease and health care professionals in good health. These factors include: hope, faith, attitude, determination, the love of life, courage, luck and chance, the ability to cope, a support system, having a purpose (or goals), and appropriate medical care. We consider the integration of these common factors to be the keystone for the will to live.

Our research began with the premise that, through telling stories of how people cope with illness or various life crises, we could better understand the process and then help to implement what we learned in our patients' lives.

Our goal was to help others, but, in the summer of 1995, we became direct beneficiaries of this research. It was at this time that Ernest acquired a rare medical syndrome, Chlamydia type II double pneumonia, and had an acute heart attack. He was on a respirator for ten days and would have died were it not for the excellence of his intensive care medical team and the love of family and friends. Not only were his own values reaffirmed, but he also learned much more about his own will to live and about the power of the human spirit.

This book deals not only with people who have faced or are facing cancer or other serious illnesses, but also those around them—physicians, care givers, and family members—who have experienced first hand or through observation some of the critical ingredients of the will to live. We believe that when you read the experiences of these people, written in their own words, you will agree that we all have an untapped potential for emotional and spiritual strength that enables us to endure.

We go through many stages as we deal with illness: fear, frustration, depression, and helplessness. We may eventually find ourselves drained by illness and inactivity, tired of feeling victimized by events beyond our control. We cannot endure such emotional upheaval indefinitely. At this point, an acceptance of reality begins to emerge along with thoughts of how to work around problems and recapture something of value in life. We consciously or unconsciously make a decision for life.

Many of the people in this book made that decision. Each of their journeys is unique, but several life-affirming themes continually resurface. It is clear that they have a message of importance for all of us.

Their stories lead us to reassess our own values and goals.

In presenting you with the ways in which others have coped, we are not advocating a drastic change in your own way of life. We only want to suggest that, even if you have a life-threatening disease, you can make choices and compromises, as you did before you were ill, and in this way live with your problems. We hope you then will increase your efforts to keep fighting.

We really know very little about this mysterious force, the will to live. It seems more potent in people who are connected to others than it is in those without strong bonds. It also seems to involve a willingness to fight and struggle through whatever the difficulties and pains of life may be.

We hope to be able to find something in those people who have a strong will to live that can be taught to those who seem to lack it. Perhaps the best we can do at this point is to share the stories and struggles of some of our patients, friends, and colleagues to reassure others that they are not alone, that their fears are justified, that hope always exists, and that attitude can make all the difference in the world.

If the contributors to this book were to give one piece of advice to those who have encountered adversity in their lives, it would be: "It's up to you. You can learn to live with it, live around it, or live in spite of it. You don't know what you can do until you try."

Ernest H. Rosenbaum, M.D.
and Isadora R. Rosenbaum, M.A.
July 1998

INTRODUCTION

By David Spiegel, M.D.

Professor of Psychiatry, Stanford University, School of Medicine

PLATO SAID that courage is knowing when to be afraid. Between the covers of this book are stories of courageous people, many of whom became very ill or faced some other crisis, yet counted—and count—themselves fortunate. In the face of a dismal diagnosis or harsh circumstances, they took stock of their resources and found strength and love.

Many of the people in this book faced sickness, but were not overtaken by it. Just because one part of them became ill, they did not give up on all fronts. Their bodies may have suffered, but their spirits remained strong.

Indeed, serious illness is a reminder that life is not infinite. Those who respond creatively to a life-threatening illness hear it as a wake-up call, a reminder of how time is short and life is precious. They do what matters most while they can, experience the joys of living and loving, and let the people around them know how much they are loved and appreciated. They trivialize the trivial, drop useless commitments, eliminate relationships that are taxing and not worth the trouble, and "just say no" to doing things they think they *should* do rather than what they want to do.

The people in this book talk about and illustrate the will to live in a realistic and meaningful way. They do not demonstrate some artificial determination to prolong life no matter what. They assess life's resources, goals, and values. They take stock and see how fortunate they are to have people who care about them and whom they care about. Mind may not triumph over matter, but mind *does* matter.

Years ago, a clever graduate student taking a statistics course was wandering through a cemetery and realized there were two types of data on the headstones: birth and death dates. She wondered if they bore any relationship to each other. Theoretically, they shouldn't. When you die, you die. Period. However, that was not what she found. People tended to die after their birthdays, not before. The difference was not large, usually several weeks, but was significant. People seem to hang on until after their birthdays or some other special event. This doesn't mean you can make yourself live indefinitely through mental calisthenics, but it does show that meaning makes a difference in the course of disease.

Another crucial theme running through this book is the power of social connection: no man or woman is an island. Prisoners of war on Bataan kept themselves alive through giving one another lectures, playing together, caring for one another.

In my own field of research, we have found that women with breast cancer help one another enormously through support groups in which they can vent their darkest fears and learn how deeply they can still care about each other. To feel embedded in a network of caring at a time of serious illness is deeply reassuring. The will to live is not the denial of death. Rather, it is the intensification of life experience which comes when you realize how finite life is.

The spirit of the contributors to this book is well captured by Carol Buck's chapter title: "I Don't Have Time Not to Live." Many people think that awareness of a serious prognosis means the loss of hope. It does not. The real issue is: hope for what? These people used their illness or the illness of someone in their family as an occasion to redefine what matters in life, to distill its nectar, and then to drink fully of it. Ruth Smith, the "tough old bird," found that in giving she got even more: "I forgot my weariness." And Laura Evans discovered in her expedition up Aconcagua how climbing a mountain is like living with breast cancer: you face your deepest fear, death; you learn the value of team support; you take one step at a time; and you clarify your ultimate values.

There is good advice in this book: be willing to make compromises, find the joy in life, find good support groups, and be partners with your doctors. These stories make it clear that we are not simply happy or sad and that pleasure is not simply the absence of pain. Illness teaches us that we can be both happy and sad and that even the threat of progressive disease and death can provide a context in which life can be sweeter. One woman with advanced breast cancer once said to me, "All my life I had wanted to go to the summer opera in Santa Fe. This year I went. I brought my cancer with me and it sat in the seat next to me. I loved it."

This book is replete with the joy of life, of people who face trying circumstances yet go about living their lives. It is inspiring reading for the temporarily healthy as well as the ill.

David Spiegel, M.D.
March 1998

TO CLIMB
A MOUNTAIN

INTRODUCTION

WHEN LAURA EVANS WAS TOLD she had only a fifteen percent chance of surviving breast cancer, she chose to fight for her life in her own way. Two years later, she reached the summit of Africa's Mount Kilimanjaro, and it was there that Laura came up with the idea for Expedition Inspiration.

Expedition Inspiration was conceived as a way to inspire hope and courage in women with breast cancer. To do this, Laura decided to lead a team on an expedition to conquer Aconcagua in Argentina, the highest mountain outside the Himalayas. The team for this expedition was a group of seventeen cancer survivors.

Many months of endurance training were necessary. It was only through courage, determination, and will power, complemented by physical training, that the challenge was met. Many of the women were undergoing cancer treatment at the time, which created additional hardships and made their efforts even more arduous. But they wanted to demonstrate to the world that, even under grave conditions, people can successfully meet and embrace major challenges in life.

Three members of the Expedition Inspiration team successfully reached the 23,000-foot summit on February 4, 1995. The other fourteen team members attained their goal of between 15,000 and 21,500 feet. This achievement was accomplished in spite of eleven days of harsh weather and winds up to one hundred miles per hour.

The team carried 170 Tibetan prayer flags, inscribed with the names of more than four hundred women who had faced breast cancer. Their goal was to raise $2.3 million for breast cancer research. This special expedition of women who had suffered or were suffering from breast cancer was a brave gesture that proclaimed to the world: "Count me in. I've got a lot more to live for and a lot more to give in this life."

The enthusiasm of their assault on the mountain, the photos they took, the prayer flags they displayed proudly at the summit, as well as each woman's compelling personal story of her climb, served as a testimonial to inspire and raise awareness around the world.

The achievement of the Expedition Inspiration team was—and is—exemplary in its own right. But it can also give courage to anyone faced with the challenge of a major debilitating injury or disease and inspire them to realize that they too can achieve their special goals. They too can say, "Count me in."

Expedition Inspiration climbers on Mt. Aconcagua

CHAPTER 1

Expedition Inspiration

Laura Evans

FOR ME, the will to live is synonymous with the love of life—love of experiences, people, places, things. I have an insatiable curiosity about what makes people tick, about what other places look like, smell like, and feel like. I am an avid reader. I love to travel. I am thrilled when I meet a new, interesting, fun person, even from a distance. And I enjoy the things I have collected or been given over the years, each one conjuring up a pleasant memory.

Laura Evans survived breast cancer with a bone-marrow transplant. She has so far climbed five of the eight major mountains in the world and led a team of breast cancer survivors in a successful climb of Mount Aconcagua, the highest peak in the Western Hemisphere.

I am an advocate for change, for pushing the boundaries of one's comfort zone. We must know cold to appreciate warmth. We must be hungry to really enjoy food. We must know death to fully understand the joy of life. I came to appreciate this more than ever in December of 1989.

Two weeks before Christmas, I was diagnosed with a rapidly advancing breast cancer. As the tests came back, my prognosis went from bad to worse. I was in shock. I had been busy living life, with a husband, career, travel, sports, and entertaining. Like many other women, I have since come to learn, I thought my life would go on indefinitely. Yet suddenly I was faced with cancer, the "C" word, the one that most often follows the word "deceased."

I was thirty-nine when I found a lump in my breast. I had never thought about cancer, and, even though the lump was clearly there, it seemed inconceivable to me that I might have breast cancer. To be certain, I went to the doctor for my first mammogram. When the doctor said, "No problem. It doesn't show anything. Go home," it was like music to my ears. So I went home. Happily. Naively.

On some deeper level when I found the second lump, I knew I was in trouble. What I didn't realize yet was that the cancer had aggressively spread to eleven of my lymph nodes and that I would be lucky to survive the next three to five years. I knew I would have to summon up all my resources. I would have to educate myself on a disease I knew nothing about. I would need to locate health care specialists who could help with both my physical and emotional needs. I would have to do something radical in terms of treatment.

I knew I was not ready to die. I thought about what my father said before he died: "No man's life is complete without his death. It is the framework for his life." But my father had done everything he wanted to, exceeding his own expectations and dreams. I hadn't. When I looked at my wish list of things I still wanted to accomplish, I was haunted by the fact that I might not get to do them. I loved my family and friends and couldn't bear the thought of not being with them, of all the great times yet to come.

With the tremendous help of my supportive husband, I took control of my destiny. We made endless phone calls to different hospitals and oncologists, finally locating a promising clinical trial in which I enrolled. I was one of the first people in the country to go through an experimental protocol that called for intensive chemotherapy followed by a bone-marrow transplant. The treatment also included two surgeries, three months of outpatient chemotherapy, and seven weeks of radiation. The transplant required that I spend two months in the hospital, seven weeks in a sterile room the size of a closet.

I almost died in isolation. The massive doses of drugs ravaged my immune system, filling my lungs with fluid. I got pneumonia and for the first time came to understand the release that comes with death. I also came to understand why I wanted to live.

As my atrophied body struggled to build itself back, my mind revisited a recent trek in Nepal that had kindled my desire to do more climbing. At night, as the sedatives to relieve my discomfort took hold, I would visualize myself standing on top of one peak or another, fists thrust defiantly and exultantly skyward. These visions, however disconnected from reality they may have been, kept me going. The vision of mountains with me atop their summits became my mental symbol of wellness, something I desperately wanted.

When I left the hospital, I was barely able to walk four blocks. But at the end of my first walk in eight weeks, I stood with my arms raised high overhead, with the hospital—and, I hoped, the cancer—a shadow in the background. One step at a time, I walked, then hiked, then started thinking seriously about getting back into the mountains. To climb again became my passion.

At the same time, I wanted to help others. Even with the tremendous love and support of my husband, family, and friends, I felt isolated by the devastating side effects of my illness. How could they really understand the mutilation of my body, and the loss to self-esteem as a woman, that accompanied the loss of my hair, the early menopause, the pain of arthritis that followed the drugs, and the emotional upheaval that left me drained and confused?

I knew that others in the same situation would understand. There was no organized support group in my hometown, however, so I started one and facilitated it for two years. Together, the women in the Wellness Group and I rebuilt ourselves.

During those two years, I gained a new appreciation for the tremendous satisfaction of giving to and helping others. I also learned how little we know about breast cancer and how little was being done. My mission became twofold: to climb and to call attention to breast cancer. And that mission became my raison d'être. I became passionate about it, and I believe that passion has kept me alive.

There is always the question of why one person survives and not another, why some people cling to life while others give up hope. I have found that the people who love life the most and live it fully have an inner fire that drives them. Whether it is golf, needlepoint, crossword puzzles, or bocce ball, it is something they clearly can't live without. I wanted to help others find that special passion and, barring that, share mine with them.

Three years after my cancer diagnosis, I realized how I could achieve that. I would organize and lead a climb up one of the world's highest mountains to raise awareness of, and funds for, breast cancer research and care. What set this climb apart was the makeup of the team: seventeen women—single women, mothers, grandmothers— ranging from twenty-one to sixty-two years old. These were not mountain climbers in the traditional sense. The only thing they all had in common, other than being women, was that they were all breast cancer survivors.

Peter Whittaker, whose involvement really ensured the climb would happen, picked both the mountain and the name of the project, while Jansport underwrote the cost of the entire climb. The mountain was the 23,000-foot Aconcagua in Argentina, the highest peak in the Western hemisphere. The project was christened "Expedition Inspiration."

Many people have asked me, "Why, when you almost lost your life to cancer, do you again put it on the line by climbing mountains? Why climb a mountain for breast cancer?" Personally, I revel in the awe-inspiring, breathtaking beauty of mountains and the satisfying singular focus it takes to climb them. The physical and mental perseverance I have to expend in order to stand on a summit demonstrates, in my mind, that there is nothing out of reach.

Far beyond what I personally get out of it, mountain climbing as a vehicle to further the cause of breast cancer awareness calls up some very poignant parallels:

■ In both climbing a mountain and dealing with breast cancer, you face your deepest fear: the reality of death.

- Each is an individual struggle that is better handled with team support.

- In order to survive, it takes one small uphill step at a time.

- In the process, you find out what your ultimate values are. You develop a greater sense of self and self-worth.

For thousands of women suffering through breast cancer, the message was clear. Many sent letters stating, "If you can climb a mountain, I can get through chemo. If you can climb a mountain, I can go out and walk a few blocks." For the Expedition Inspiration team members, it reinforced what facing a life-threatening illness can teach you: that too often we walk through life unconsciously. There is, in reality, no time to waste. Now is the time to go for it.

The Expedition Inspiration team—the first true national support group—alleviated some of the fear of "joining the club" by demonstrating that getting a cancer diagnosis does not necessarily mean your life is over.

Through Expedition Inspiration, we helped educate women not just about breast cancer, but about themselves. I have met few women who are not hard on themselves. Most of us give endlessly, forgetting about our own health and well-being. With this project, we wanted to empower others to let go of what doesn't contribute to their wellness and to applaud their own talents and interests. We wanted to teach the importance of knowing our limitations without limiting ourselves.

Through the Expedition Inspiration Fund for Breast Cancer Research, which includes ongoing international expeditions as well as locally sponsored Take-a-Hikes, I have dedicated myself to helping others. I have written a book, *The Climb of My Life**, to encourage others to follow their hearts. I feel as if I have been given a special gift—the gift of life—and I don't want to squander it.

But I never lose sight of what rejuvenates me, what sparks my will to live. So I take frequent forays into the wilderness, always finding the solace or answers I seek. I look for the laughter, the irony in all things, realizing how infinitesimal we are in the much bigger picture. I remember to laugh out loud daily, sometimes for no apparent reason.

On rainy afternoons, I reevaluate my wish list. What else do I want out of life? What else can I do? Ten years from now I won't look back and say, "I wish I had _____." Ten years from now, I'll have a new wish list of all the great adventures yet to come. There's so much to live for.

*Laura Evans, *The Climb of My Life: A Miraculous Journey from the Edge of Death to the Victory of a Lifetime* (San Francisco: Harper, 1996).

CHAPTER 2

To Call Forth That Spark

Kathleen Grant, M.D.

AS AN ONCOLOGIST, a cancer doctor, I am always thinking about helping people define their will to live. Individuals with families often define this in terms of their relationships, as in, "I've got to see my ten-year-old daughter grow up."

Those who don't have strong relationships or gratifying careers may have a more difficult time marshaling their energy. So, they need to be empowered as individuals. It's important to develop a sense that "you are important because you exist." The healing bond between a physician and patient is in part an expression of hope and the will to live, in which the physician is saying, in effect, "You are valuable as an individual, and I want you to get well."

Hope is part of that empowerment that says, "I have a right to wish for more life, more health, more time to accomplish a goal." The goal doesn't have to be a physical achievement. Even a determination to look good after completing chemotherapy and to start dating again is an expression of life force. Each person needs to find a way to express this feeling.

It is important to distinguish between a person's physical limitations and his or her desire or ability to express life. Someone who has to have a lung removed for cancer can still have the same vitality, even though that person is probably not going to climb a mountain.

In January 1995, I served as one of the team physicians for a group of women breast cancer survivors who climbed the 23,000-foot Aconcagua Peak in South America. Called Expedition Inspiration, the purposes of the climb were to raise hope, public awareness, and research funds.

I was very worried about the health problems that might arise in this group of cancer survivors—problems related to either their breast cancer or to their previous treatments. Being at high altitude is risky anyway; even completely healthy people can get seriously ill or even die at altitudes like those we were going to attempt. I was very preoccupied with watching for signs of illness, but remarkably little went wrong.

After the extensive chemotherapy and radiation treatments the women had received, the climb was an incredible physical achievement, never done before under such circumstances. Beforehand, there was no way to predict whether it was going to be safe or successful. One woman had a couple of bad days because of her arthritis, a side effect of her chemotherapy, but she was still able to complete the journey.

The opportunity to be on the climb helped many of the women to be less emotionally and physically passive. Some of the group had never really done anything physically challenging before. One woman had three "firsts" on the first day of the trip: she had never been on horseback before, and we had to cross a river by horse the first day; she had never slept in a tent overnight; and she had never urinated outdoors. This is a woman who is very daring and forceful in other ways—she's an attorney and certainly knows how to get what she wants—but participating in the climb opened up another dimension of what her life could be like.

For this group—and from what I have seen in caring for other cancer patients—just being alive is not enough. There is a need to continue achieving and stretching the limits. The determination to prove themselves physically was especially striking in the climbers. Many of the women talked about "taking it to the edge" and about how their diagnosis had changed their priorities, challenging them to experience events as vividly as possible.

I wanted to challenge and prove myself physically as well, because I've had some serious health problems—cancer and multiple retinal detachments. My participation in Expedition Inspiration, both as a climber and as a physician, helped me to further define my own goals. It certainly made me want to climb more mountains. I was obsessed with mountain climbing when I came back from that climb, and I'm still trying to figure out where that fits in my life.

Some of my favorite moments on Aconcagua were at night, when it was so quiet. At high altitude stars seem very close, and it was very calming to feel linked to the entire universe, despite our campsite being only a small dot in the landscape.

One of a physician's roles is to foster the will to live—to call forth that spark—by giving patients examples of others who have done well and helping them find their own uniqueness in their period of crisis.

One of my patients with very serious breast cancer was hospitalized for her bone-marrow transplant the evening the documentary on Expedition Inspiration was shown on television. She wrote to me from her hospital room about the tremendous confidence watching the broadcast gave her for her own future.

I think the will to live is a natural component of being alive. All animals have it, and I often think of its source being in the primitive, emotional parts of the brain rather than the intellect. When you are not challenged by the fear of dying, it's all too easy to just kind of "sleepwalk" through daily routines, always getting frustrated at the little things in life. The threat of actually having life taken away can make a person suddenly want to prove a point to the world, or to change direction. Risk taking, physically or even emotionally, is part of that. The fact that this group of women, who had gone through chemotherapy and radiation treatments, were able to achieve this physical feat should make them justifiably proud.

I heard a priest-philosopher give a lecture a number of years ago. One of his points was that clinging to life was not good, and that at a certain point patients should move from hope to resignation. He described a woman with advanced ovarian cancer who talked with him about her goals and hope for further life. He didn't consider her a candidate for active treatment, but she focused on getting more chemotherapy.

The priest said to her, "Why do you want to do that?"

She said, "Well, at least it would give me hope."

"Hope for what?" he asked.

She looked at him and said, "Well, just hope."

She did receive further chemotherapy but died a few months later, apparently heartened by her belief that all appropriate therapy had been tried.

Hope is such a tiny word, because we throw it around and can't quite get to the kernel of its meaning. In many ways, our hope is for continued existence, for feeling alive. In oncology we really see very few suicides, perhaps because people have already come to grips with the precariousness of life, despite the paradoxes and painful moments.

The will to live is so strong and primal that it is a rare person who is ready to move on, away from life. The wish to remain, to be, is enough.

UNFINISHED BUSINESS

INTRODUCTION

IN HIS 1951 BOOK, The Will to Live*, Arnold Hutschnecker, M.D., wrote: "If we truly wish to live, if we have the incentive to live, if we have something to live for—then no matter how sick we may be, if we have not exhausted the last of our physical resources, we do not die. We live because we want to live. But the incentive must be one in which we inwardly, utterly believe. It is not the 'everything to live for' in the eyes of the world that keeps us alive, but the something which meets our own uncompromising measure of what is worth living for."

Many seriously ill people manifest the will to live because of an upcoming special occasion or a desire to achieve a goal: the birth of a grandchild, a final birthday or holiday, the completion of a novel, a mountain they haven't yet climbed. Physicians often observe a phe-

*Crowell, 1951. (Reprinted by Simon & Schuster, 1986.)

nomenon—called "the Christmas syndrome"—when a very ill person decides that he or she wishes to live to enjoy another day that has always been special for them, such as a holiday like Christmas.

This section explores the lives of three seriously ill people who had unfinished business that galvanized their will to live.

CHAPTER 3

Each Day Really Is a Miracle

Father Isaacs

I LOOK BACK on my twenty-five years as a priest as very happy years. I would never change them. I've had wonderful experiences. I went to Peru for five months as a missionary and then went to the mountains at Lake Titicaca. I went to Curaçao and Machu Picchu.

I am now stationed at a large, Hispanic parish in San Francisco. My story of cancer started about three and a half years ago when I was diagnosed with a melanoma on my back. I had an operation and it was removed. The doctors said they'd gotten everything and there probably wouldn't be any more problems. But three years later it came back, which was extremely shocking. I've always believed that when you get rid of something, it's gone.

The first sign of the recurrence was that my left side became paralyzed. I thought I'd had a stroke. I could hardly walk and couldn't use my hand. I held off seeing a doctor because my twenty-fifth anniversary in the priesthood was coming up, which was an important event. But I couldn't make it. My condition just kept getting worse and worse. My speech was getting slurred. I went to see my regular doctor, who did a test and said, "No, you didn't have a stroke. You probably have something far more serious."

I had a brain scan, and the doctor scheduled surgery to remove a tumor from my brain. The surgeon gave me some time. He said there was no rush and that I should have my party, and he gave me some very powerful steroid pills to reduce the brain swelling.

I walked out of the hospital and down the street to a Catholic church that had a statue of St. Jude, a patron of the apostles. I went in to pray to him. I planned on being very impassive about this whole thing. I said, "I'm not praying for health. Whatever God wants is no problem."

The day before I went in for my operation, I had my "twenty-five years ordained" party. It was a huge mass, with tons of people, choirs, and dancers. At the end of mass, I asked for peoples' prayers. I went into the hospital full of confidence.

The tumor was large, the size of a silver dollar. The neurosurgeon was quite confident that the tumor was encapsulated (confined to one area, not spreading throughout the body), so for the second time I thought, "Well, that's it. I'm finished. I don't have to worry. I can go back to work and forget it."

But later, I had another problem. The surgeon explained that it could be either a recurrence or a residual bit of tumor they just didn't get out. I had a small amount of radiation and, so far, everything has been fine.

In the midst of all this, between seeing doctors and feeling very confused, I read a very helpful book, *Choices in Healing** by Michael Lerner. His basic premise is that you have to call up your own healing powers, which seems obvious, but it was totally new to me because I had never been sick. Soon after, I met with Mr. Lerner, who recommended a book by Lawrence LeShan, *Cancer as a Turning Point*†. This happened to be the right book, at the right place, at the right time. There were a couple of stories in there that were just dynamite. Reading it was a turning point for me.

Lerner said the question isn't, "What's wrong with you?" Instead, the more appropriate questions are: "What would be truly healing for you in your life at this point? Short term and long term, what would be right for you? What is it in your life that you like? Who are you? How can you help yourself to do more of what you find truly fulfilling? And how can we help you to keep doing that?"

The will to live, I believe, has to do with finding the place in your heart where you are, where you live, and realizing that you have not yet accomplished all you wanted. It is awakened by looking through a new set of eyes at what you have been doing and getting a new perspective on your life. For me, it involved not denying the past but realizing I had to deepen what I'd done and start to get back on track with my goals.

After the radiation, I went back to the church near the hospital and

---

*MIT Press, 1994.

†Plume Books, 1994.

prayed again. This time I said, "I want to live. I have a couple of projects, and I want to do them."

This time I didn't say, "Whatever God wants is no problem." It's not that I don't believe in God's will anymore. I still do, very much, and it's very important. Whatever God wants, obviously, is the bottom line. But to me, the heart of life is not just us discovering the will of God. It's God asking us, so that our will can become aligned with the will of God.

I said to God, "If you ask me what I want, I have a plan and here's my will. If it's Yours too, okay. If it isn't, okay. But here's me."

I laid out very clearly what I wanted in my heart. And I felt a jump. I felt that I was heard. It was a moment of recognition. I felt it was going to be up to me. If this is what I want, it's going to be up to me to get it. This isn't a rehearsal. We're not here just to sort of see what other people need. We're here to do things, and if God has given us some insights, then we need to realize them. Otherwise when we die He can say, "You didn't do what I wanted you to do."

I prayed, first of all, to be able to complete a collection of stories I started writing fifteen years ago. I've written short stories all my life— just quick, unpolished things—but I had never put them together. I even used to write down conversations at somebody's house or a phrase or a word. I have one enormous file called "Exactly" that's filled with stuff that I heard and that made me think, "That's *exactly* right." So I'd write down whatever it was and put it in the "Exactly" file. A lot of my stories came out of that file.

While I was recovering from the brain surgery, I finally got the stories all typed up, bought a word processor and did some correcting. I was very happy writing them.

The other part of my prayer was to say, "Here's what I really want for the parish: to tighten it and give it a vision."

My parish is in the middle of the Mission District and is a very, very busy place. We have a congregation of over two thousand people and the number of religious services is extremely high. Apart from the masses, we have six to seven hundred baptisms a year, and a huge number of weddings. We have fifty people a night sleep in a shelter, several youth groups, a clinic with doctors and dentists, a theater group, a religious school with over five hundred children, and an after-school program for about four hundred children not going to Catholic schools. It's a massive project in terms of administering a million-dollar-a-year budget. None of us were trained for such a task, so, needless to say, there are a lot of pressures.

I now have to pursue my vision and let the chips fall where they may. I try to make as many changes as I can to alleviate some of the pressure. I don't have time to please everybody, which is what I think I tried to do before.

There are some things I've always wanted to do with the parish in terms of hiring different people, giving it a new direction, and bringing the social and religious, the social and spiritual, together. I think I have now deepened the direction of both.

I wanted to bring in more Spanish culture through music, plays, and sociodramas using liturgy for teaching moments with theater. We started celebrating the feast days in the same way our parishioners celebrated them at home, so they wouldn't feel lost or like strangers. It gave them more of an ownership of the parish. We painted a big mural—which won awards—on a church wall, so that when people walk by they could stand up straighter with pride rather than feeling beaten down. Since the cancer and since my moment of recognition, I think I have deepened my understanding of these projects.

I had another experience, another moment of recognition, in the middle of this whole thing.

I always lived very fearfully. I guess that goes back at least as far as the seminary. There were so many rules and so much fear. That was just part of my life. Life and death were so frightening. When I first got this thing, this cancer, I was so frightened. I remember going into a restaurant and physically feeling my heels digging into the carpet under the table in fear.

Then, just before another operation, something happened. I can't explain it, but my fear just lifted, and I thought, "Whatever is to be." The fear left me. There wasn't anything to be worried about or frightened about.

Someone once said, "Worry is interest paid on money you'll never see." I understand that now. "This is life, this is death, and I'm very much part of it. Whatever is to be."

All my life I've handled problems by working harder and more. In that sense, my life hasn't changed much because of my illness, but everything has been greatly clarified. I think I'm coping with things the same way I always have, but some insights have become a little sharper, and I've cut out a lot of the nonsense of life.

When I got sick again and it was suggested I get my affairs in order, I thought of not going back to the parish. But I decided it was no use sitting around, worrying about what might happen. I decided to find a path that has a heart, and that path for me is back in church, working with people, and directing my parish.

I have learned so much about God and about prayer and my spiritual life. I've had much more time to pray.

I now feel like I'm beginning to be able to competently guide people. Sometimes I wonder what I said before, because I don't think I knew anything then. Whatever I knew was probably very superficial. Maybe it was out of a book, and maybe it was right. I hope to God it was. But now, I'm very conscious that guidance has to come, somehow, from within. If it doesn't come from the heart, it doesn't work. Now I really know what I'm saying, and I mean it.

I always considered myself a very hopeful, optimistic person. But there was a time when I used the word "exasperated" a lot. That word came to my lips quite often when the tumor was growing. When I thought of what was happening to me, I used to sigh. I never felt so exasperated. That's when I fell apart.

But now, I've been re-reading a lot of books I've enjoyed over the years and have felt physically and mentally better. I read Hamlet, Macbeth, and King Lear again, and they kind of pick me up, give me some new ideas, and help me get back up and on the trail again. I've been seeing people I haven't seen in a long, long time. I've been enjoying each day. Each day really is a miracle. People say that, and you hear it, but it's not until you experience it for yourself that you know it's true.

Looking back, I'm so happy I had the opportunity to look at myself, to stop and see what I wanted to do in terms of this little part of me, this little inner part. I feel like I'm in a good place in my life, and I feel this is a great time to say I have a vision about what I want to do with the parish. And I'm going to do it.

Before I knew how serious my illness was, I was planning to take a trip after my twenty-five year anniversary, perhaps back to Peru or Ireland, or maybe to Italy, whose beautiful churches I have never seen.

But what I realize is that, since my party and my operation, I had a much more wonderful year with far more extraordinary experiences than any vacation could bring.

Now when I think of having missed going to Peru or Ireland, I just laugh. I would have gone, come back, people would have asked how was it. I would have said "wonderful," and it would have been over. Two months later I would have forgotten I had gone.

Now I say, "I've had one of the best years of my life." And I really mean it.

Father Isaacs with his mural at the parish in the Mission District in San Francisco

CHAPTER 4

Arms Too Short to Box with God

Val Staton

MY CAREER has been as a dancer at Finocchio's, a female-imperson-ator club in San Francisco. I've performed as Sophie Tucker, Marilyn Monroe, Dolly Parton, Mae West, Rita Hayworth, and Wynona Judd. I'm thirty-three years old now, and I have AIDS.

I define the will to live in terms of the desire to continue on, to see what's around the corner, and to have some semblance of a nor-mal life.

The pleasures of life add to the will to live. I enjoy theater. I enjoy reading. And I enjoyed acting very much. It was still a job, but it was nice to work at something where I got to smell good and wear spark-ly-colored evening gowns.

I got into it when I was very young. It was the only way I could actually get into the clubs. I had a baby face and, back in those days, all it took was some mascara and lip gloss and I was a woman.

There are things that have boosted my will to live. Getting some good news about getting well I would definitely rate as number one. Comfort level is very important and could be number two. To be able to eat again is definitely on my wish list, even though all my life I've been heavy and have desired to be thin.

My grandmother is fond of the old expression: "Where there is life, there is hope." But there's another expression: "I'm tired of all that's ailing me and of not dying." There is only so much a body can take. The awful thing about AIDS is that when you just get over one thing, then there's immediately something else to knock you down.

You can be totally decimated. I didn't have the ability to eat, to feed myself, to get myself out of bed. I did nothing but vomit for nine and a half months and had temperatures between 103 and 106 degrees.

There has to be a time when you decide to give up. The body can only sustain you for so long, and you can only take so much. I have been with more than 180 people when they died, and there is a point when you can look at them and tell whether they're ready to go. It's been said there comes a time in life when death becomes a friend. Death is just as natural as a shower.

Yet even when you're emotionally ready to die, there is an almost spiritual spark that just won't let you go if you're not really ready. That spark allows you to go through the bone-marrow taps, the surgeries, and the excruciating medications you have to take.

The will to live is intrinsic in us as human beings. I think it's what keeps people going after tragedies, holocausts, disease, and whatever else. With AIDS I may be losing my *battle* to live, but that doesn't mean I'm necessarily losing my *will* to live.

One of the things I take comfort in is the fact that life is going to go on. The day I die, people are going to walk down the street and go to their jobs, and they will continue to do it for as long as mankind is here. That's life. It's somebody else's life. It's not yours. But it goes on.

You can get to a place where you think there is no hope, that there is no quality to life. I was there. I tried to cash in. I was willing to die, to just give up because of the excruciating pain. I attempted "euthanasia" twice and failed. I am alive, I think, because of my will to live. And I am also alive because my higher power did not want me to die.

I am convinced that a lot of the will to live is based on our own sense of pride. But along the way we lose our pride and say, "Okay, it's your will now, not just my will." You can't just do it on your own.

My will to live is God's will for me to live, because if God wants me dead, my ass is cooked. Like that great musical called "Your Arms Are Too Short to Box with God."

I believe very strongly in the relationship between myself and a higher power. I live out my personal relationship with God. God is somebody who directs me and has a purpose for me in His universe. It is for me to discover what that purpose is.

I basically went to the "wall" and tried everything to stay alive until something finally did work. Protease inhibitors came on the market and saved my life. As far as body weight goes, I went from 220 pounds to 120 pounds by the time I finished the course of drugs. Now I weigh 162 pounds. I am very happy with this weight.

There is a fifteen percent failure rate with the protease inhibitors right now. It's not a magic bullet, but it's the closest thing we have had in the fifteen years since this health crisis began. I am very fortunate to be one of the people who is a true success story. My doctor says I have had one of the best responses to the protease inhibitors of any of his patients. I am basically back to normal.

Now I get up every day, try to do thirty minutes' worth of exercise on a Stair Master and eat just about anything I want. I am not concerned about the quality of what I'm eating, just the quantity. I eat all the ice cream I want. As I say, I used to beat myself up because I had a weight problem, but not anymore.

My experience with AIDS has completely changed my direction in life. I am not sure what I need to be doing yet, but a lot of things happened to me when I was so ill, including near-death experiences and going deeper into the more spiritual side of my life. The whole process was excruciating. I wouldn't wish it on my worst enemy. But it has also been the most enlightening and maturing process I have ever lived through.

When she was dying, my mother told me, "Nothing matters in life but life itself and those who you love. The rest is bullshit." If I could make one statement, it would be, "Nothing matters in life but life itself and who you love." I have a sense of peace about me now that I didn't have before, a sense of spiritual comfort. And when you have internal comfort, it is a lot easier to tolerate outside discomforts.

I've lived my entire adult life with HIV. I've lost many, many friends and some lovers to this disease. It has been a genocide of my peer group. I have gotten some comfort and knowledge out of reading things by holocaust survivors, people who have dealt with this kind of multiple loss and trauma and had to face their own mortality at the same time.

Yet, after being devastated physically as much as I have been by this disease, it is really incredible to actually look with hope towards a halfway normal life expectancy. It is also scary.

The great thing about having gone through what I have gone through is that we will all have to go through it again. I'm going to end up dying from something some day. Hopefully, it will be old age. But I don't have to be afraid of dying anymore. Dying's not scary.

The will to live can overcome anything and, if it can't, it is because it is not meant for you to overcome it. You have a purpose in your life and you have a purpose in your death. There is an expression, "Let go and do it by God."

You can have all the money and material possessions in the world. You can be totally secure financially, but, if you are dying, you are in the same boat as somebody who has nothing. A person who has their basic human needs met and has the comfort of faith and the ability to accept and continue on is much better off than somebody who is only materially wealthy.

I haven't worked in three years. Instead, I've been living off of disability. Now, instead of just going back to work, I am thinking about going back to school. I want to be a nurse. I was inspired by the home care nurses I had. I wouldn't be alive if it hadn't been for their compassion and their positive reinforcement, their attitude of, "You're going to make it. You're going to be okay."

There are other things I want to do too. Being an entertainer has given me the ability to deliver a message. There are many people in the gay community who still have not been tested for HIV. There are many who have been tested and, because of denial factors, don't seek active medical care. I want to be a positive role model for people in the gay and lesbian community, particularly in the HIV community, as someone who has accessed good medical care and been successful with the available drugs.

I'm glad my attempts to leave life didn't work. I am grateful that I am alive. I have something to learn and something to give. I believe that God has a higher purpose for me. I don't know what it is as yet. But it will come to me. It will be revealed.

CHAPTER 5

I Don't Have Time Not to Live

Carol Buck

WHEN I WAS GIVEN my diagnosis that I had a possibly fatal malignancy and I had to take chemotherapy in order to live, it didn't change my style of life at all, except that I of course got tired. I pretty much knew even before I saw the doctor that I had breast cancer because of the physical signs, the shape of the breast, and so on.

I wasn't angry when they said that the breast was probably going to have to come off. Angry isn't the right word. I was mad at being inconvenienced by it.

The operation and the subsequent treatment of chemotherapy and radiation obviously took their toll on me but didn't really change my lifestyle a whole lot. I had complete confidence in my doctors, and I just knew I was going to get over it and get through it.

My doctor's care and encouragement were extremely valuable to me. Every time I went to see him, I got a hug and was told how nice I looked. Such support is wonderful, such caring. A doctor can be very important, as far as making you feel that you're still a woman, that, even with breast cancer, you're still going to come back.

At my fifth treatment, my doctor, Alan Glassberg, looked at me, no hair, no nothing, and he said, "You're not your same cheerful self. What's the matter with you?"

And I said, "I don't know. I just don't feel too good."

"Which treatment is this?" he asked.

I said, "My fifth."

"Ah," he said, "it usually happens at four." He gave me a big hug and a kiss and said, "Get in there and get it over with."

After that, something inside of me said, "You're going to be all right."

I remember, finally, one day about four months after I had finished everything, I woke up in the morning and felt like myself again.

At my next meeting with the doctor, I told him this, and he said, "Well, you look like you did back when I first met you."

My nurses were also incredible, especially one named Irene. If I could have made Irene a saint, I would have. To me, she is the one who most helped me through everything. I've watched her with people who were not going to get better, and her kindness is incredible.

I think I had such confidence in what was happening to me, the treatment that I was getting, because of the positive attitude of my doctor, Irene, and everybody in that office who cared. Even the girls out at the front desk cared. They made me feel like I was part of the family.

It is also very important to trust the people who work with you. From the first moment I walked into my doctor's office, I trusted him. He told me what he was going to do, and I said, "Okay, that's fine. Go ahead and do it tomorrow." Trust is very important.

There is a great connection between the mind and the body. Whatever brings you joy and pleasure, relaxation in life, whether it's reading or watching old movies, listening to opera or jazz, or playing with the grandkids, you have to have that in your life. Especially when you're fighting something like cancer.

I've been through several other accidents that have almost killed me. And each time I survive one of these things, I have an even stronger feeling that there is something more for me to do before I go. I often don't know what I need to do specifically, of course. Some of it has to do with my involvement with opera and with education and scholarships. But I know there's something out there I still have to do, and it will present itself.

My strong will to live is based, I think, on the fact that right now I'm too busy to die. I'm doing too much, things that I feel are really important in more than just my life but also in other peoples' lives. I had been doing that for about ten years prior to coming down with cancer, and I'm still doing it: helping others enjoy life.

So, I still feel that I just don't have the time. I don't have time not to live. I live a very busy life, both in life and in enjoyment.

There's no time to sit down and cry. I've never had time in my life to sit down and cry, and I didn't when my breast cancer was discovered. I certainly got depressed, but I had wonderful support from my family. My son said, "Hey, Mom, come on. Let's go do this." All my golfing ladies said, "Well, come on, you'll probably hit the ball better now, when you get your strength back." That sort of encouragement is important.

I don't know where my certainty of not dying yet came from. I'm not a very religious person, but I did sit down and pray before I started my treatment. I asked God to let me get through, and I asked Him to help me not get too sick. And He answered my prayers. I had the great fortune of never having any bad side effects.

The best way I can summarize my feelings about the will to live is to recall an incident I had right after my surgery. I was sitting across from a woman who had cancer and who was scared to death. I looked at her and said, "Hey, I'm okay. I'm shooting for ninety-two, and I'm enjoying life." That's not bad.

PUTTING ON THE BOXING GLOVES

INTRODUCTION

ALL PEOPLE, not just the critically ill, face grave moments in their lives. We have all, at one time or another, been tempted to give up and not continue. During these tumultuous times, it's often easy to miss the opportunities for what could be very rewarding achievements.

Consider a story about Niccolo Paganini, one of the great violinists of the eighteenth and nineteenth centuries. He was giving a concert when one of his strings suddenly snapped. Although the audience gasped, he continued playing. A second string broke, and, without missing a note, he continued playing. When the third string gave way with a sharp crack, the violinist momentarily stopped playing, but he then continued with persistence and confidence. He raised his Stradivarius above his head and announced, "one string...and Paganini." Then, with tremendous skill and discipline, the gifted artist finished the selection on a single string with such perfection that he received a standing ovation.

Like Paganini, we need courage, dignity, and optimism to meet our challenges in life with hope that we can overcome whatever obstacles are present.

Indeed, life-changing obstacles often become catalysts that awaken or deepen our will to live. Illness or other crises frequently force people to step back from their day-to-day lives and ponder the meaning of their very existence, wondering about the purpose of their life, contemplating why they want to survive, and then firming their resolve to do so.

We are always impressed by the spirit and grace with which people cope with chronic disease, disability, and the threat of death. We have seen again and again how they refuse to let debility or discomfort affect their enjoyment of family and friends or prevent them from going to work or pursuing outside interests. Inspired by their fortitude, we asked them how they were able to transcend their problems, what made them want to live.

The answers we received at first seemed simple and obvious: My children, they said. Or, my grandchildren. My wife. My husband. My dog.

But there was more to it than that. As we listened to their stories, we realized that the will to live means that they really *wanted* to live, whether afraid to die or not. They wanted to enjoy life, they wanted to get more out of life, they believed their life was not meant to be over, and they were willing to do whatever they could to squeeze more out of it. After a period of feeling devastated, they simply decided to assess their new reality and make the most of each day. When it came right down to it, they simply loved life and all it has to offer.

The threat of death often renews our appreciation of both the importance and transiency of life, love, friendship, and all there is to enjoy and learn. We open up to new possibilities and begin taking risks we didn't have the courage to take before.

Many of our patients tell us that facing the uncertainties of living with an illness makes life more meaningful. The smallest pleasures— eating dinner by the fire, walking the dog, the smell of fresh-cut grass—are intensified. Much of the hypocrisy in life is eliminated. When bitterness and anger begin to dissipate, there is an even stronger capacity for joy.

One patient wrote, "I love living. I love nature: being outdoors, feeling the sun on my skin or the wind blowing against my body, hearing birds sing, breathing in the spray of the ocean."

Yet another said, "I, like many others who are ill, went through a period of anguish and decided, yes, life is still beautiful, still precious and—until the last breath—worth fighting for. I have learned to truly value life, to cherish it, to enjoy it and appreciate its bittersweet brevity. When you make the momentous decision to live, you suddenly find that you never knew how to live life fully until you faced the reality of losing it."

CHAPTER 6

A Broken Window Every Day

Maria Smith

I'VE HAD TWO extremely good fortunes. One was my husband, Donald, a remarkable man with whom I had a magical marriage. The other was my oncologist, without whom I would not have survived. Any other doctor would have looked at my prognosis and said, "It's over!" I was given a gift with the two of them, and something in me used that gift. Subconsciously, I didn't think I could fail either one of them.

If you have confidence in those who care about you, then you can go through a lot of stuff. You go on with life with real strength. I had a lot to support me. Would I have done it had I been a single person? I'm not sure. I think one of the worst things is for people to go for treatment every week and feel that they're in a cold, steel world. My husband and my doctor alleviated that. I always felt that I had a comforter around me.

In 1970, at the age of thirty-three, I had a mastectomy for breast cancer. Later that same year I had a hysterectomy and an oophorectomy (surgical removal of the uterus and ovaries). One morning I said to Donald, "Let's talk about this. Do I have a chance with what's going on here?"

He said, "That's entirely up to you." That's all he said. Not, "I can help you," or, "your doctor can help you." Rather, "it's entirely up to you." I think I took in that message and decided that there was no reason for me not to be positive. What did I have to lose?

My surgeon, Sheldon Levin, also said something very important to me. It was the day before I left the hospital and my family was supposed to move to a new house. I was kind of down and said, "I want to ask you. We're about to move. Should we?"

He said, "Don't change anything, keep on going." It was a simple statement that helped me. He has been a major support over the last twenty-six years. I have often called him several times a week just to talk.

In 1971, I was told I had advanced breast cancer with liver, bone, and lung metastases. My doctor put me on chemotherapy right away along with an experimental immunotherapy program, BCG, a tuberculosis vaccine and Transfer Factor, a mixture of immunological chemicals. I later had eight weeks of radiation to my back. I didn't know how I was going to do it, but I did it. I had a three-year-old daughter. There was a lot I was fighting for.

Once I got over the pain and my body started to heal, I made an effort to get out of bed every single morning as if nothing were wrong.

I'm not sure my thinking was even that specific. I just had a lot of "crutches" around me, and I was very much in love. I never even thought about it, I just got up out of bed and started the day. That was a gift. That was God's gift.

Chemotherapy was something else. The first time I had chemotherapy, it was devastating. I had to block out a day every week for I don't know how many years. When they'd shoot those drugs in my vein, I could feel them going through my whole body. Immediately, psychologically, I'd become ill. I would go home, prepare dinner, then just go to bed and try to block it out until the next day. I wasn't really very good at it. Donald wouldn't allow me to stay in bed. I'd have to get up and sit at the table. The food would drive me up the wall, but I did it.

Donald also made me get films from the American Cancer Society. Every single day for an hour, I'd set up a movie projector on the dining room table and watch a film about how cancer cells migrate, how they kill, and how they are killed by lymphocytes in the immune system. I don't know what that did, except that it was a hell of a chore.

I went to a support group once and wanted to wallop the participants. To me they were a bunch of whining women talking about losing their breasts. They drove me crazy.

One thing I found that helped was that I never cried in front of my family. I discovered very quickly that if I had an emotional breakdown in front of them, I not only had to lift myself up, but I had to bring all of them up too.

So I just broke a window every day. Sometimes more than one a day. That really got rid of a big thing inside of me. I decided that if I ever wrote a book the title would be *A Broken Window Every Day*. After a few weeks, the window repairman asked me why I was doing this. I told him I was really angry. He didn't ask me any more questions after that.

Another important point is that I live in a small town, and a lot of gossip was circulating about me. So Donald went to our tennis club one day and told everyone to mind their own business. I didn't have the energy to deal with someone calling every day wondering if I was going to die. There were days that I looked so horrible people must have known something was going on. But I made a conscious decision not to go into any detail with anyone. That privacy was a tremendous help.

I went to the dentist and had to fill out a form about my health. I wrote "excellent." Where it asked if I had any diseases, I put "advanced breast cancer."

The dentist came out and said, "Are you serious?"

I said, "Very serious." That was the end of the conversation.

It was like being an actress on stage. I just went on with my life. I entertained. We took trips. With my daughter where her schooling was concerned, my activities were limited because my immune system was so weakened. So I chose to do all the carpooling. This kept me seated and let me use as little energy as possible. But it kept me in control of the kids. That was important because I didn't feel detached from her growing up.

I took ten years of chemotherapy and concurrently three years of immunotherapy. The tumors in my liver shrank significantly, and then my treatments were changed to hormone therapy. My doctors tried to compare my old nuclear medicine scans from 1970 to new CAT scans in 1980 only to find out that my old scans from 1970 were not available. The doctors didn't keep x-rays over seven years and they thought I had died, so they simply tossed them out. I was on various hormonal therapies for about eight to ten years, and then, because of the progression of lung metastases, I was again placed on chemotherapy with a complete remission of the lung tumors.

In 1994 I suddenly lost my major supporter. Donald died suddenly of an acute heart attack after returning from the tennis club. It was the most devastating event of my life. Although my mother lived with me, I felt alone for the first time.

Even if you're doing fine, there's a medical check up on your illness every three months. The worst one was the first one I went to alone after Donald died. I thought I was going to give up the treatments. Now I'm going at it on my own and it's okay. I think I've resigned myself to the fact that I'm either going to be able to make this work a while longer or I'm not. If I'm not, I'll start the countdown and cease treatment.

In 1995 my doctor wanted me to go on Taxol, which meant I would lose my hair again. Actually I did a very bad thing once which didn't turn out so badly. I was on Cytoxan and finally got so disgusted with the thought of losing my hair again that I took myself off chemotherapy for a few weeks. When my doctor heard about that he almost finished me off himself right then and there. Fortunately it did not hurt me.

Faith has been very important to me. I don't follow any organized religion, but I've always believed in God and that's been a source of much strength. But I've always been a strong person. My father had one expression when there was a problem: Handle it. He said, "You've been prepared to handle it, just handle it." I've relied on that strength too.

Dr. Rosenbaum

Maria had an amazingly strong will to live and phenomenal endurance throughout her twenty-six-year battle with cancer. Even when she realized she was fading during the last few months of her life, she did not wish to discuss her future with me. She always kept some hope that she would get better. When asked how she wished to be cared for, her only request was that she should be made comfortable and be allowed to die in peace. She would even lie to her daughter Leef—who was twenty-seven years old and a newspaper reporter in Washington, D.C.—about her declining health. Maria did not want to worry her. While they talked almost daily by phone, she maintained that her health was stable.

In April 1996, Maria began to develop a left-sided weakness. She was unable to get about on her own and had her ninety-year-old mother to help her walk rather than admit that she needed help. She asked her mother not to tell anyone about her failing health.

She became progressively worse, but she didn't want to go into the hospital or see a doctor. Isadora and I were in Europe for two weeks. She refused to have a hospital bed with a trapeze or wheelchair. Her primary physician, Marcie Gotlieb, M.D., ordered a home health nurse and blood tests which showed an elevated calcium level reflecting her advancing cancer. She improved only a little on medical therapy.

On the day we returned from Europe I had a message to call Maria. I called, and she said, "I'm going to die today. I've been waiting for you to return. Could you come over to see me?"

When we arrived, I found her toxic and mentally lucid, but dying.

We had a meaningful conversation, discussing her life and attitude, and she thanked us for our care over the last twenty-five years.

She said good-bye to her family and the special people she loved and died shortly thereafter.

There is a will to live and also a will to die. Maria exemplified an amazingly strong will to live. When Donald died, Maria lost a major life force that had promoted her own will to live. She decided that she did not wish to begin using Taxol, a new chemotherapy treatment, which two years before she and Donald had been excited about. When she decided she could not live with all the disability, discomfort, and pain and could no longer take care of herself or her mother, she decided to die. She was always a proud person and could no longer accept that her illness had taken away her dignity.

Leef Smith

Fighting cancer consumed nearly half of my mother's life. It was her enemy, her nightmare, and, ultimately, her greatest secret.

Only a handful of people ever knew that the strong, outspoken woman they loved was battling disease. Even her closest friends, the ones who drove her to chemotherapy each week, were in the dark. Sure, they thought it was odd, maybe even suspicious that she went to the hospital, and of course they asked if she was okay. My mother knew they were on to her but she tossed off their inquiries with what she believed was a plausible excuse. She told them she was on the board of directors at UCSF. It was a lie. It was also her protection story.

"Why?" was the question on everyone's lips following my mother's death. Given the secrecy surrounding her illness, it was a death that hit friends and neighbors like an unexpected blow to the head.

Just hours before her death one of my mother's friends called looking for her. "I'm sorry," I told her, trying hard not to cry. "My mother isn't well, She can't come to the phone."

"Oh, I know Maria has the flu," she persisted. "Just put her on the phone. It'll only take a minute. I want to touch base."

"No really," I said, my grief turning to anger. "She's dying. She may only have a short time to live, and I can't talk to you right now."

"That's crazy," the woman said. "We talked last week. She's fine."

A friend rescued me from the remainder of that very surreal conversation but many more like it followed in the days after my mother's death. No one could understand that she had died and they were angry, angry that she hadn't let them help her when she clearly needed it. Some of them felt betrayed.

But she wanted privacy. It was her sanctuary from the disease. It allowed her to survive in the workplace without speculation and emotional injury and to focus her attention on fighting the cancer. She wasted no time battling peoples' perception of her as a victim because few people knew about it. Some would say that medicine kept my mother alive and seemingly healthy for so long. Certainly modern medicine had a lot to do with it. Just as important, though, was her will to live.

My mother was a fighter. She fought every battle on her own terms, and those terms centered on privacy. She was asked several times by her doctor to speak to breast cancer support groups, but to her those women were holding the ultimate self-pity party, and she would have none of it. If my mother had a mantra, and maybe she did, it surely would have been "I am not a victim." Rather than risk being treated like one, she chose to hide her troubles from her friends. And, when it suited her, sometimes from her family too.

Sometimes when my mother and I would have arguments, my father would say, "Don't you realize how sick your mother is?" The answer, really, was no. To all intents and purposes she always looked healthy. No one would dare talk about it. Unlike today, cancer was something you hid from the world, not something you reveled in beating. Whatever else you can say about it, this strategy worked for my mother. Between her trust in the Christian Scientist belief, "mind over matter," and the unfailing love of a devoted husband, my mother held off the disease.

The flip side is that until my father's death, I was pretty much out of the need-to-know loop regarding my mother's health. She and my father made it their goal to shelter me from the reality of her condition. That was fine, until suddenly I needed to know.

Clearly what stopped her was my father's death. He was her number-one support and confidant. Without him, she was scared and alone. While I believe my mother would have given anything to see me married and to hold my children, she also knew I was now a grown woman with a bright future. She knew she could let go when the fighting became too much.

As her condition deteriorated she kept the news from me, her friends, even her ninety-year-old mother. At least in my case, it wasn't so hard to do. She lived in California, and I kept a home in Virginia.

While it wasn't my mother's intention to lie to me, more important to her was a lifetime spent minimizing her sickness. Admitting to me that she was really sick meant admitting it to herself. After twenty-six years of fighting successfully, she couldn't admit the truth.

My mother asked me for one thing before she died. She made me promise that I would neither purchase a death notice in the local San Francisco area newspapers nor hold a memorial service.

My mother lived for twenty-eight years in an affluent town in Marin County where she was a well-established realtor and social butterfly. I wanted to honor my mother's wishes. I thought long and hard about the appropriate course of action. In the end, we held a private service at her home, but I was too proud of her struggle and her strength to deny telling the Bay Area about her.

CHAPTER 7

Realize What's Important

Darrel Ansbacher

1974

I THINK TIME is something man invented, and it really is in some ways one of our greatest inventions. In other ways it's the scariest. It gives you a beginning as well as an end. If there's a chance of that end being premature—for instance, if you have a potentially fatal disease—there is no gamble too great to take to get rid of that disease. You don't worry about whether the cure will be worth it.

My point of view is from someone who's on the homestretch, who has a chance of cure, and I'm speaking as a nineteen-year-old. But my advice to anyone who is considering treatment is that, as long as you have time, as long as you have the gift of a normal life ahead, there is nothing you can do that you can't try to undo later. The cure will be worth it.

After what I've gone through to hold on to life, not to fear death would be a mistake. But I don't think my fear lies in the childish fear of death, in fear of the unknown or darkness or being alone. My fear is more like paying an exorbitant price for a piece of jewelry and then being afraid of not getting the jewel. It's as though I don't deserve death yet. I've paid the price. I've bought time. I deserve life.

Philosophy is not that big of an issue when everything is going OK. Philosophizing about life is something that matters much more in a crisis, so for me to define my philosophy right now and pinpoint how I feel about my body and my vulnerability is difficult.

I'm more aware of every ache and pain. There's a fine line between hypochondria and hypersensitivity, but one of the best ways to describe hypochondria after you've had some sort of cancer is that you live a life in which there are no bumps, only lumps. You jump to the conclusion that every little thing that gets raised on your body is not a bruise or simple swelling—for example, from bumping your knee on the table—but is some sort of growth.

I still have lots of visual reminders of my treatment. There are scars, but not just the one on my belly from surgery. There are my eyes, which protrude as a result of damage to my thyroid from radiation treatments. There's the balding hair on my temples and the little patches missing here and there in my beard. I still notice these effects and have acclimated myself to them without ever really getting used to them.

But as to whether I have made any decisions differently because of cancer, I'm not sure. I'd like to believe that I think things out a little more carefully than I did when I was younger, but that could partially be a result of just getting older.

The only thing I can really say I have now that I don't think I would otherwise have had is that no one can confront me with a situation and say, "There is no way you are going to make it." I have confidence that any set of circumstances can be dealt with.

All the promises you make to yourself in the last two months of chemotherapy about what your perspective is going to be on the day it's over don't always come to pass. The whole time I was taking chemotherapy, I thought, "Boy, when this is over, those petty little things that used to bother me just aren't going to bother me any-more." That's true to a certain extent, but it's also true that when you get better, you have the same anxieties and problems you did before, and you still have to cope with them.

Disease in many ways is a method of avoiding coping with a lot of your normal problems, inadequacies, and insecurities. As long as you're sick, you can forget about them, because, of course, the reason for your problems is that you're sick. When you're well, they'll be gone. In fact, when you are well, everything is just as burdensome and there are just as many crises and as many meaningless "what-am-I-going-to-do" things as there were before.

But I like to think that, in a real pinch, I would feel that as long as I have time, I can straighten things out and that, comparatively, the crisis at hand is not that bad.

I've also changed in another respect. I find I don't worry as much about things that would have made me very nervous before, for example, the rent being overdue or being late for an appointment. I've had something in my life that was *really* worth worrying about.

I saw my friends during this last quarter at school panic when final exams came around, especially the premed students. I don't say this to their faces, but I wonder what disease they're going to have to get before they realize what's important in life. I find my own grade-point average is higher because of this attitude. I take things much easier.

I don't know what I'm going to do yet, but, unlike my fellow students, if I don't have a job when June rolls around, perhaps that's not the end of the world. I'll just have to keep looking. I don't know whether Hodgkin's disease took the edge off my competitiveness, whether I'm characteristically a less competitive person, or whether I have a better sense now of what is important and what isn't.

I wish I had a chance to talk to prospective employers about Hodgkin's disease during my interviews, because I consider it to be one of my greatest achievements. Some people climb the Matterhorn and afterwards they show slides and want everyone to know about it. I'm sorry there's not a place on my resume to show I had Hodgkin's. After all, I survived that a lot longer than I've held any job.

I understand the stigma that's attached to a sick person, however, both in his own eyes and the eyes of an employer. For the prospective employee, it's rather like the person who is embarrassed about seeing a psychiatrist. He hates to show any weakness. Even if he is open about it, other people may think of it as a weakness. A person who's looking for a job doesn't want anyone to know they've faltered because some people in the business community think people are born to success, or not. Are you going to be a lucky guy? Are you a guy who lives a charmed life, or are you going to be a loser? If you were just on the operating table for four hours, maybe you're a loser.

I look at it in quite the opposite way. I think the real winner is the guy who was on the table for four hours and lived to get up off of it.

I view what happened to me as a malfunction and believe the technicians pretty much corrected it. What enabled me to get better as comfortably as I did was having my family around. I had people to feed me, help me walk around, and pick me up at the hospital. I was lucky not to be the guy who showed up for his chemotherapy on the bus then went back to his apartment alone in a cab. That doesn't mean such a person can't get well, but it must be much more difficult.

I think endurance is important. I don't know how to develop it, but all my life I've had methods of getting through unpleasant things. The hot coals are there, but you just look at the other end, close your eyes, and walk over them—just do it. Like when I wake up in the morning and have to get out of bed, I have a swinging technique so that no matter what my mind and body say, I can get my feet on the ground. You are looking at that spoon that's filled with God knows what and you know you can swallow it.

That kind of endurance takes on uncommon importance when you have to go into one more radiation treatment. While you're taking off your clothes, you focus on being in the dressing room afterwards. You remind yourself of the last three or four times you were there, and you think about getting dressed again. That's all you think about. Not about going to the Bahamas when you get well. If you've been successful at everything you've done in life and have that kind of endurance, then maybe you will feel a little better about your chances of fighting cancer.

I think the will to live is a crisis mechanism you don't know you have until you need it. Part of the will to live is endurance and part is resourcefulness. But a lot has to do with having the imagination, when things are really bad, to divorce yourself from what's going on. When you really want to live, you'll think of ways to work at it, no matter what the situation.

1998 Update

The past can't be changed. Nevertheless, when offered the opportunity to revise the above passage which I wrote almost twenty-five years ago, I was tempted. But I can't change those thoughts and observations anymore than I can be that age again. Instead, I will add this brief postscript.

Like any nineteen-year-old, nobody could tell me much of anything. My beloved parents blessed me with a solid ego that often led me to state my opinions as if they were the wisdom of the ages, when they were nothing more than the rantings of a teenager. Today I am much less sure of things. I am wary of people who seem too sure of simple answers to complex problems as well as people who are convinced that life's answers have somehow been made clear to them while the rest of us search aimlessly.

Some physical scars are permanent, some transitory. The same seems to be the case with emotional scars.

"I'll never be the same."

"If I survive, I promise I'll never _____."

"If I survive, I promise I'll always _____."

These are conclusions reached in a foxhole in the heat of battle. Twenty-five years later I am overwhelmed by the normalcy of everyday life. All such promises and expectations seem to have drifted into oblivion.

Charles Dickens' story of Scrooge is built on the faultiest of premises. It presumes that the experiences of one night can fundamentally change someone from sinner to saint, from schmuck to mensch. No matter how dramatic the events, I would argue that, by definition, the natural state of affairs is normalcy. Scrooge would inevitably fall back into old patterns and come to rest somewhere beyond his old self, but also short of sainthood.

So it must be with those of us who are long-term cancer survivors. Fundamentally changed? Yes. Candidates for sainthood? Give me a break! In any case, no matter how much if any "personal growth" results from having survived this disease, it would have been far better never to have had it.

I am left with fundamentally the same tools as everyone else with which to confront life's hurdles. But perhaps there is one tool in my arsenal which not everyone can claim. Somewhere deep inside, I suspect I could endure cancer treatment should it, God forbid, ever reappear.

In fact, I did have a reoccurrence of cancer. Not in me, but in my father, who ten years ago was diagnosed with prostate cancer. When he thought he couldn't face another treatment, he once told me he found strength in remembering how I persevered during my treatment many years earlier. If this eased his suffering by one iota, then there is definitely something of some lasting value in having had cancer myself. His death two years later overlaid my own successful cancer cure with a profound understanding of the tragedy that remains all too common an outcome for many cancer patients and their families.

There is no "blessing in disguise" here. There is just the chance to live each day, drawing upon the past, hoping for the future, and trying to appreciate the journey which so many years ago almost came to a premature end.

CHAPTER 8

A Tough Old Bird

Ruth Smith

1997

BACK IN 1982, when I was fifty-eight years old, I went to different doctors because my leg was bothering me, and I was unable to walk. It felt like a screw was going in. None of the doctors could find out what was wrong with me, and I was beginning to wonder if my pain was in my head. When I was on crutches and unable to walk, my orthopedist wheeled me into UCSF/Mount Zion Hospital and said, "We're going to find out what's wrong with you from the tip of your head to the bottom of your toes." I never will forget that.

He said he was going to find the answer to my problem if it was the last thing he did. He couldn't understand why I couldn't walk. So an evaluation was done which included CAT scans and mammograms.

The mammogram showed a shadow. A breast tumor was suspected, and the biopsy turned out to be cancer. The orthopedist called me on the phone and told me that he was going to have a doctor, an oncologist he knew, give me a call and see me soon.

When he said that, I laughed, and he asked what I was laughing about. I told him that I knew the oncologist he was referring me to. That very doctor had looked after my sister about five years before when she had lung mesothelioma, an asbestos-related cancer, and he did a good job with her. I was just happy to be in somebody's hands that I already knew.

When the oncologist came in, wearing his white coat, he said, "Your orthopedist told me to come in and talk to you about the test results."

I asked the doctor, "Don't you know me?" and just laughed. The seriousness hadn't really taken hold of me yet.

After he looked me over, he said, "Ruth, you know what? As long as I'm able to do anything for you, you won't die of this tumor. I'll do everything I can." That sounded like pure gospel to me.

After the lumpectomy, I had radiation therapy and chemotherapy. Over the years, I've had excellent care, and I could have had no better doctors. Even today, when I come into my doctor's office, I forget what's wrong with me. The positive attitude I get from him and his wife gives me the strength to keep going. They give me hope.

One time, I fell asleep in his office. When I awoke I wrote, "Hope is the companion of power and the mother of success."

The cancer recurred in 1995, but it took me some time to realize it. I don't fault my doctors or the testing they did at the time, because I wasn't listening. Your body tells you one thing, but your mind is elsewhere. I was too busy at the time to really notice what was going on with me until it surfaced in an eruption of cancer lumps.

On my first visit with a new surgeon, he was very straight with me about my treatment. I was scheduled to have a double mastectomy, with the potential removal of part of my chest wall (sternum and ribs). He looked at my age, my health, and the facts that I've had so many surgeries and so much happen to me through the years. He told me all the possible problems I might have if I was on the surgical table.

My daughter was present, sitting off in the corner crying her heart out. She asked, "Mom, do you really want to go through with this?"

It was up to me to make the decision, and I didn't say a word until the doctor finished. I thought, my goodness, out of all the doctors over all the years, this one here doesn't pull any punches. I challenged him by saying, "Doctor, I was referred to you by my oncologist as one of the best. I'm not putting you on the spot, but I believe that if you do what you're supposed to do and this works, then fine. If it doesn't work, I'm not holding you accountable, because God's going to be in the room with me. I'm a God-fearing person, and I know that whatever you do, God's going to be taking care of Ruth Smith. Okay? And if I don't make it, it's not your fault."

He said, "You know, Mrs. Smith, you're a tough, old bird."

I said to him, "I'm going through with the double mastectomy and chest wall surgery. If you don't do it, I'll go home and take a butcher knife and do the job myself." I have to admit I like to joke around and have a little fun. But I did believe that, with the help and the inspiration of my good doctors and God, I could make it. I wasn't going to give up.

On the first anniversary of that surgery, I was seventy-two. My plastic surgeon did a fantastic skin graft, which also gave me a "tummy tuck." I think I wear my clothes very well since my radical mastectomy.

My life is dedicated to helping others make it. My life is not over yet. I've had a lot of chances not to be here today, but with the help of God and my doctors, I'm still here.

I've had a rough life. I was a single mother with three children, so I had to work hard. But I've had good spiritual guidance, and it helped that my father was a strong man. I give him credit for my being as strong as I am.

When my children were teenagers and I was a single parent, I strove for them to have an education, something I didn't have myself. I didn't go past high school. All three of my children were educated through college.

I have a beautiful family that is very devoted to me. I helped one child go through private school on scholarship. Professionally, my children are successful. One of my daughters is the Director of Operations for the Department of Public Works of San Francisco.

I have no time to sit down and worry about myself, Ruth Smith. My phone rings constantly. I'm usually not at home. I just let the door slam me in the back as I leave. When I'm having my bad-feeling days, I get out there on the streets. I just keep going. I don't sit around and mope. I'm very independent and outspoken.

I am the senior member of a group of women I work with, and they don't want me to give up either. A lot of them get low in spirit and will not take the reins and go on. I'm trying to give them the reins. They're younger; they're more able, but they won't do it. If I'm not there, the clock will stop ticking. This actually helps me to go on. I have a lot of children out there. All these ladies are my children. Some of them are in their forties and fifties.

I'm also an advocate for out-of-home placement of children. I speak for those who can't speak for themselves. I counsel families that are desperate in one way or another—about their kids, their husbands, and the struggles of everyday living. I encourage them by telling them about my experiences and how I would do it. "Don't give up," I say.

What gives me the will to live? My family, my God, and my interest in children and people. I have a lot of goals. Trying to find happiness is one of my goals, and I have found it within myself and my children and other families. Every weekend, I talk to my mother's family and my aunts. They all call me or I call them, so we have a network. I like that. I like networking with my family, to keep in close contact with them. I love to be with people. I like to share things with them.

I wrote a little poem today while I was waiting for my doctor. It kind of summarizes the way I look at things.

Today, I sang a little song and I felt my heart grow light
And walked a little mile with not a cloud in sight.
Today, I smiled and things didn't look so bad.
Today I shared with everyone else a bit of hope I had.

Today I worked with what I had, didn't long for any more,
And what had seemed like hours with my family at my door.
Today, I loved a little more, complained a little less.
And in the giving of myself, I forgot my weariness.

1998 Update

When I'm depressed, I get out of the house and go and let the door hit me in the back. I go see friends and talk about other things and try to forget my health problems.

I'm on the San Francisco Department of Human Service's "Family Preservation Committee," which helps keep families together. It's a struggle to get anything done with the bureaucracy.

When I'm up, I just keep doing everything I can; and when I'm down, I talk to my nurse at the doctor's office and get a lift. I'm trying to get over this illness, but I do slow down at times. I plan to do good as long as I can move.

Last week I came to a committee meeting and everyone got up to give me a seat, but there was a seat in the front which was available.

Then I was asked, "How did you get here?"

I answered "I drove." They just could not believe it. They were amazed and surprised. But I like surprising people who think I am already "six feet under."

The will to live? It is knowing that you can do something for someone else. That keeps you going.

CHAPTER 9

I Live a Disease-Threatening Life

Rick Fields

WHEN THE DOCTOR called to say that the biopsy had come back and that it was positive for cancer, my first reaction was that I felt like I was in the middle of one of those World War II movies where the Zeros are attacking the boat, the sirens are going off, and everybody is jumping out of their bunks and rushing on deck and all sorts of explosives are going off all over the place.

Rick Fields is a Buddhist practitioner. He is the former editor of *Yoga Journal,* a contributing editor to *Tricycle,* and the author of *How the Swans Came to the Lake, A History of American Buddhism.* Portions of this chapter originally appeared in interview form in the Fall 1997 issue of *Tricycle: The Buddhist Review.*

That was my initial reaction. And it was an accurate one, because this cancer had been undiagnosed (not that I hadn't tried) for over a year. So it had gotten into a very dangerous place, and I really did have to do something pretty aggressive and drastic about it.

But the thing is, you never know what's going to happen. You could have a car accident on your way to some wonderful healer. It's actually one of the basic Buddhist teachings. Part of the practice of one school of Tibetan Buddhism involves repeating the Four Reminders. One of the reminders used is: "Death is real. It comes without warning. This body will be a corpse."

So it's part of my Buddhist spiritual practice to really understand that. It seems that human beings have a sort of automatic shut-off valve having to do with their own death, even though it's pretty much the only thing that's certain, except for our birth. The certainty of our death is the one thing that everybody ignores.

There's even the possibility that much of culture and civilization is organized to help us ignore death. So, from that point of view, a terminal illness can be very helpful to your spiritual practice.

By chance, the same evening when I first learned the results of my biopsy, a Medicine Buddha teaching was being offered. Part of this teaching is that when you have sickness, it's a great opportunity to take on the karma of the sickness of other people. This is very different from the Western notion of getting sick, because it turns everything all around. Basically you imagine that your sickness is you taking on the sickness of all other people in the world who are suffering in the same way so that they can be free from their suffering.

The idea is to take any situation that occurs to you and make it part of your spiritual path. It's not just good situations that become part of the path, but *any* situation. So the situation of illness also becomes part of the path.

When later on I spoke with other Buddhist teachers, usually the first thing they would say was, "Well, you understand of course that everybody has to die, that death is real." Rather than lead in with, "We can cure this and you'll be alright," or, "Say this and it will heal you," there was this kind of very bare recognition that, "Well, what do you expect? You were born, so you're going to die." Almost like, "Yes, what's the big deal?"

A little deeper than that is the idea that, "You're lucky because it's good for your practice. You have time to prepare for this." Whether you are a Buddhist practitioner or not, if you are a human being you have time to prepare yourself. The usual notion in the West is, "Oh, so and so is very lucky that they died in their sleep or they had a heart attack or a sudden kind of thing." But here's the idea that cancer is particularly good because you usually have some period of time to contemplate the whole thing and to work with it.

The first doctors that I saw all asked me, "Do you know what the percentages are?" The statistics for stage-four metastatic lung cancer, which is what I have, are not very good. And, once I found that out, when they would bring it up I would tell them that I wasn't interested in hearing about it. What good would it do me?

I don't see what value it would be to have someone say to me, "Okay, you have four months to live." And anyhow, I don't want to give that much weight to any one person's opinion, whether they're seemingly an enlightened spiritual person or a super Ph.D. M.D. I'm not convinced that what they see in either case is accurate or even helpful.

Basically, my response to my cancer always is, "I'm going to live until I die." Which is all anyone can do. Whether you tell me I have four months to live, or three years, or five years, or whatever, I'm going to live until I die.

I told one of my doctors, "You are also going to live until you die. You think that you know when I'm going to die. You don't even know when you yourself are going to die."

The Buddha pointed out that everything that is born will die. Death is real, it comes without warning. We don't know when it will come. And this body, this particular body, will be a corpse. Buddhism has always been very consistent in looking at that.

The first doctor I saw had the idea of doing a little treatment, palliative stuff, and then for me to go trek in Nepal or go play at St. Andrew's golf course in Scotland. Go play! The immediate feeling seemed to be that you've spent your life and haven't done what you really wanted to do, so now you should go play golf or go trekking in Nepal or whatever it is you really want to do.

And I told him that I had done what I wanted to do, more or less. And it's not like I'm now going to take a vacation. I've done with my life what I wanted to do, for better and for worse, with all the ups and downs. And I'm going to continue to do that. So what are you talking about? I'm going to fight this. And if I die fighting it, fine. I'm going to die sooner or later anyhow.

The doctor said, "Really, it's a philosophical more than a medical question. The question is whether you want to emphasize quality of life or to be very aggressive in treatment." And that was sort of a code. What he meant was, if you do a lot of chemotherapy and radiation, which is what you would do to aggressively fight the disease, then your quality of life might not be very good, and you might just be making yourself sick and miserable.

And beneath that is the message that we don't really know, we don't really think it's going to work. We think maybe we could prolong your life for a certain amount of time, but prolong it in a way that's so disabling that the question arises as to whether it's worth doing, or perhaps we just do a little bit of treatment so you'll have four months of relatively pain-free and misery-free existence in which to go play golf or do whatever it is you want to do.

So my first decision with this oncologist was, which path did I want to take? Because he didn't want to take responsibility for either path, since he couldn't say to me, "If you do this radiation or this chemotherapy, you'll be better." For all he knew, I could go through all that and not get any better. But when he understood that I was willing to take the responsibility for my own treatment and to make that decision, he relaxed. When I said, "No I want to fight this as aggressively as possible," he was able to acknowledge that that was my decision and help me do it.

Then there was the question of whether to do the radiation and the chemotherapy at the same time. There was some idea that the two can work together synergistically, that if you do them both at once, the effect is stronger, but at the same time, the side effects can be more serious. The statistics on whether it really was more powerful to do both at once were somewhat ambiguous.

My question was "Will the treatment kill me?"

He said, "No. Even if your white blood cell count goes way down, we can give you something that will bring it up; and if you get so sick you can't eat, we'll feed you through a tube; and if your hair falls out..."

Well, I didn't worry about that! Being a Buddhist and having your hair fall out isn't necessarily a problem. So I said, "Well, it seems that if I don't do something kind of drastic, the cancer is likely to kill me, so let's do it."

Both he and the radiologist advised me against doing the radiation and the chemotherapy simultaneously because they believed the side effects I'd be going through would not be worth what might be a slight medical advantage.

My Chinese-Jewish doctor, who was my advisor on this whole process, thought it was worth doing. So I was in the odd situation where my so-called alternative practitioner was recommending that I "pull out all the stops" of conventional medicine, and my conventional people were being much more cautious.

I decided to do it. I had to do something. It felt like something had invaded me. Of course, it was my own cells that were doing it, so there was also the idea that it was a part of me. Even so, my first response was definitely a warrior energy towards this cancer which I felt I had to fight.

I remember using visualization, particularly a kind of a Buddhist wrathful-deity visualization, and a wrathful mantra while the radiation was working on me, visualizing the cancer cells being destroyed.

I went for a massage after the first radiation treatment, and I was in kind of a state. Of course they were giving me steroids for the cancer that was in my brain, and I didn't quite realize their effect at the time, so everything was feeling more intense anyhow. I had been sleeping just a couple hours a night. I was in Berkeley getting a massage, and this person who was massaging me took it upon herself to be some kind of healer. She said she could feel a lot of fear in me, and I said,

"There's no fear in me."

She said, "If I could just make a suggestion: if you had more love in your heart towards your cancer, that would be a better thing."

And I rose up and bellowed at her in a kind of rage, "No!"

She backed up against the wall, shaking.

"I'm not coming to you for that!" I told her. Kind of like, "F_ _ _ off." I didn't say that, but there's this sort of New Age spiritual idea that you should love your disease, and while that can be appropriate at times, this was not one of them. I was facing something quite serious that was trying to kill me.

Once I was driving by myself and I put on a Hindu devotional tape. It wasn't mind-boggling or anything like that. But I just started weeping at a certain point. And that gave way to this tremendous explosion of anger and rage which came out. I just started screaming as loud as I could because I was in the car by myself, which for Americans is like a place of meditation and refuge, a cave, a confessional. And here I was driving down Nineteenth Avenue surrounded by everyone else doing their thing in their car. And I was screaming at the top of my lungs, "F_ _ _ you cancer! F_ _ _ you cancer! Cancer F_ _ _ you!" I ended up writing a whole poem called "F_ _ _ You Cancer," and that was a very powerful moment for me, just to be able to express that feeling.

I was angry at this thing that had come and taken over my life. Or tried to take over my life. Another battle that goes on is making such a big deal of it and putting it at the center of your life.

For a lot of people dealing with cancer, or dealing with any kind of illness, it takes a tremendous amount of time and effort and energy. At different times, depending on how threatened you feel, it tends to take a central role in your life. It's like this whole other project added to the project of living in itself. Your life is kind of organized around this thing. That's a big shift; that's a big difference.

And that's one of the major things I resent about it. That you end up relating to doctors and hospitals and tests and taking medicine and all this stuff assumes a central organizing principle in your life. I sometimes resent that. And then I remind myself that this is medicine I'm taking. But I resent it.

So that somehow has to be kept in check or in perspective because otherwise the disease has won in a completely other kind of underhanded way by taking over your life, by being what your life revolves around. It's not the central organizing principle of your life. The central organizing principle is what you make it. For me, it's awareness or Buddha-nature. My anger was more a rage at realizing how much it had usurped my life in demanding attention like some screaming two-year-old brat.

All these things, all these emotions, pass through your mind. The question is whether you allow them to become the determining factor of your action in this moment, and I think that's something that Buddhist training and study really helps with. There could be anger and still today I wonder about lawsuits against certain doctors who didn't diagnose me correctly.

When my doctor looked at the reports, he saw certain tests that particular doctors hadn't done, possibly because of insurance things. He said, "This is a real shame." He said he would have been angry. He asked me, "Aren't you angry?"

And I said, "I don't see that anger against these doctors is going to help right now in what I have to do."

I've found that it's not unusual to be underdiagnosed. And now I can see that I was in some ways complicit with that because I too readily accepted their assurances. From what I have learned about the medical world, both conventional and alternative, I basically don't trust anybody. It doesn't mean that I don't work with people as closely as I can, but I don't assume that this person, whoever they are, knows the answer. Because it's clear nobody does know the answer.

I learned that the prognosis was considered not very good, statistically speaking. But I learned something else from a young doctor at Stanford, where I went for a second opinion. He told me, "Everybody says this is incurable. We have no way to cure this once it gets to this stage." And then he added, "Has anybody said to you 'incurable' does not necessarily mean 'terminal'?"

I said, "No, nobody has mentioned that." And it was true that in my own mind when somebody uses that kind of language, I'd jump to terminal. He said there are lots of diseases that are incurable or chronic but can be lived with or managed and are not necessarily terminal. I was going to get a T-shirt that said "Incurable but not necessarily terminal" on it.

I had about six months of remission. Remission means of course that the instruments cannot detect anything. That's all that it means. Technically. And if that goes on for five years, supposedly you can relax a little bit more. So there was a period of remission.

When I was in remission, the image that came up for me was that cancer, or whatever disease it is, is like a rhinoceros. Like you are there and off in your peripheral vision is this rhinoceros with these beady, ugly, red eyes and leathery skin and tsetse flies buzzing around it, with one nasty horn, like an evil unicorn or something. And that rhinoceros is more or less peacefully chomping on the swamp grass. So as long as the rhinoceros is chomping on the swamp grass and not noticing you, you're fine and you're in remission, but at any moment the rhinoceros could look around and turn its head, and you might be making some sort of move that would attract the rhinoceros' attention, and at that point it goes crazy and comes at you. So you are always living with this pet rhinoceros, even when the cancer is supposedly gone or is in remission.

But before my period of remission, when I was combining radiation and chemotherapy, what they said would happen did happen. For a while I couldn't eat, and I was being fed intravenously, and I was also hospitalized for a few days because I ran a little fever, and they were worried about infections.

I had my Buddhist practice materials with me, and I was meditating during that time in the hospital. I wasn't meditating all the time, of course. I was also reading magazines, visiting with people, having needles stuck in my arm. But I always had my meditation practice materials right there. I had a picture of one of my Buddhist teachers and I had a representation of the Medicine Buddha.

I remember one particularly bleak moment when I was in the hospital and a nurse came in and said, "If your white blood cells don't come up, and it looks like they are not coming up, we're going to have to put you in complete isolation." That's where when anybody comes into the room they have to have gowns on and all that.

I remember thinking, "God, this is just what I was trying not to have happen, and now, by going against what everybody was saying, instead of dying of cancer maybe I'll just die of some stupid infection because I have nothing left to fight it with." And, it being a hospital, the main support for patients is a television set that's mounted up there in the room. So I turned the television set on.

It was about three in the morning. The dark night of the soul. I had turned the set on, and I was just watching some really stupid thing. I can't even remember what it was. It might even have been the Shopping Channel. I was feeling really bad, and then I just turned the television set off and started my meditation practice as well as I could. And that made a big difference. That was kind of a turning point. When I had reached this nadir, what I turned to, rather than entertainment, was practice.

A lot of people wouldn't have that choice at that point. Recently I was in Los Angeles, and just off the highway there is a large Virgin Records superstore that has this big sign that can be read from the freeway: "If entertainment is your religion, exit now, exit here!"

That seems like such a perfect sign of the times. I don't think there was any irony there in that sign. That's basically what our religion is: entertainment. When you go into hospitals, what they have there for people is a television set. That's the religious, spiritual support people get. In every hospital room, that's there. Distraction. That's what kids have. If you are in the waiting rooms, that's what's going on.

My experience with spiritual practice is that quantity is related to quality in a certain way. The quality of your meditation deepens with the amount of time you actually spend doing it. I would say that facing death or living with a life-threatening disease probably works out to at least a couple of months in retreat time in terms of concentrating your mind.

This isn't a particularly Buddhist experience. In the eighteenth century, Samuel Johnson said, "The prospect of hanging wonderfully concentrates the mind."

When you are facing death, you start to look at things, and you know it's not a question of when I get this done, or when that happens then this will happen later. It's being here right now. And that's what spiritual practice seems to be about, continually bringing you back to the "right now."

It didn't matter how long I was sitting in meditation, as long as I could connect with my practice, on the spot rather than necessarily going and doing something else. It doesn't change just because you have cancer. The same things happen as happen with anybody's meditation. You go in, you go out, you get bored, you have insights, you have good times, you have bad times. It's not a matter of the result necessarily. The meditation practice is the whole point; you're not interested in a result. It's very hard to describe. There is a sense of, not so much what's important, but what's unimportant, I think. You look at the world and see people suffering over such silly things or creating suffering in such ways and you wonder, "What are they doing? It doesn't make any sense."

It's not like when you get cancer you become something other than what you are. I still have habitual patterns and delusions and illusions, and I get sucked up into life. The deeper questions become, "What does it mean that I am going to live until I die? What does living mean?"

Allen Ginsberg called and reminded me of something that one of our Buddhist teachers had said to an acquaintance of ours who had had a really hard life and was about to undergo a liver transplant. Before he went in for the transplant, this teacher told him, "If you live, that's good. If you die, that's good. Both are good."

I don't want to make my death into the enemy. Because death is not the enemy. Death is part of us, it's part of our life. It comes along with birth. So, if death is the enemy, then we're really in a state of very extreme alienation from ourselves and the whole process of life and birth and death and everything.

So I think there's a lot of confusion there. Death is not the enemy. Cancer can particularly be seen as the enemy at different stages or at different points. But death itself, however it comes, or whenever it comes, is not the enemy. It's something to be embraced in a way. And that's really the true warrior's stance as far as I understand it.

When samurai warriors went into battle, they carried a little purse containing the money for their funeral and everything that was necessary. If you go into a battle fearlessly accepting the possibility of death and almost embracing it, you have a much better chance of fighting well, and in fact of winning, than if you go into battle scared of death. I think a lot of Buddhist and spiritual practice in general is aimed at removing the fear of our own death. The fear of our own death is like the fear of our own birth or the fear of our own life.

When my recurrence happened, my doctor said, "Your disease is atypical. So I'm not sure how to treat it."

"What makes it atypical?" I asked.

He looked at me and didn't say anything. So I said "You mean it's atypical because I'm still alive?" And he shook his head, "Yes."

I've been very fortunate in terms of preparing for death because one of my teachers has given instruction for a yogic way of dealing with death. If you are trained in this way, then you continue your practice during your death. The way to train for it is really no different than training with your meditation in life. It's not like there's some big, secret, complicated, yogic things to do when you die; you simply continue your meditation practice at the moment of death.

I asked this teacher a question about pain killers—would it be better not to use them and so on. He laughed and said that shouldn't be a problem. For one thing, if you are feeling a lot of bodily pain, it's harder to practice and concentrate. Actually, when the body and mind separate, there is so much general confusion and chaos in that moment that it would be very difficult and not even very useful to keep your consciousness.

Our Buddha-nature has survived so much. Through countless lifetimes it has survived the fires of hell, of drowning, God knows what. Buddha knows what. It survived. So a little morphine isn't really going to affect your Buddha-nature; don't worry about it.

I've found that to be a useful teaching. The idea is that Buddha-nature is unborn and therefore undying. So to practice with that as the ground, and that as the path, and that as the fruition seems to me the best thing to do.

Death is a very personal kind of thing. Everybody has their own death. When you realize how personal it is, you know that, for each person, death in some way seems a continuation of their life. People tend to die in somewhat the same way that they have lived. If somebody has lived by sweeping everything under the rug, then they might prefer dying with the complicity of everybody saying, "Everything's going to be okay. Don't worry, you'll be out soon."

Death is not the enemy. Everybody has their own death, and to treat death as the enemy is to be in a state of complete alienation from your own life. If death is the enemy, then everybody is ultimately a failure because they will lose that battle. When people battling cancer or any disease see death as the enemy, they feel that they have failed in their fight.

It's a tragedy for people to have that put on top of all of the suffering and the struggling that they are going through, to feel that they have failed and didn't do enough, didn't do the right thing, that they didn't eat the right low-fat foods, that they didn't drink enough wheat grass juice, that they didn't uncover their shadow side, that they didn't go psychologically deep enough, that they didn't quit smoking. That they didn't meditate enough, have positive enough thoughts, all the endless guilt-tripping that people can get into.

The fact is that no matter what we do, no matter how much we do, everything—as the Buddha said—everything that is put together will come apart. Everything that is born will die. And there's nothing wrong with that. That's part of the way things are. Meditation is partly about realizing the mind, that is beginningless and therefore endless and open and luminous and has been called deathless. But that has nothing to do with what happens to the physical body. The physical body does die. And that death is not in any way a failure. It's a logical culmination of our life.

Of course there's fear, but there's nothing wrong with fear. We keep having these ideas about what is spiritually correct, and that's really unfair to people. If I'm afraid, then I'm afraid. So what? Who's making out the report card?

Investigate fear, go into it. Don't be afraid of the fear, but rather be curious. Be exploratory. How solid is it? It feels very solid, obviously, because people freak out about it, but if you lean into the fear and investigate it, you know what it is actually made up of. It's made up of these physical sensations, which, when you direct awareness or attention to them, tend to lessen or dissolve. It's made up of projections into the future about what's going to happen or what's not going to happen. So the arising of fear, if you have a spiritual practice, actually can be a very powerful kind of aid to the whole spirit, to your practice. You can use your illness or any situation as an aid to practice. There's nothing that will occur that cannot be seen in that way.

One of the Buddhist practices that has been emphasized by teachers to me again and again has been "tong-len," which is to breathe in your own situation or your own fear or your own pain and fully feel it, to take it in and not try to push it away, but then to breathe out a meditative calm and extend that to people you are close to, whom you love, who are undergoing the same kind of situation, like people in my cancer support group or people I know personally who are suffering more than I am and are really struggling. And from there, the practice is to try to take in the suffering of all sentient beings who are struggling with disease and illness and the fear of death and doctors and insurance companies. The whole thing.

The idea is to bring all of that in and to breathe out a sense of calm and equilibrium and confidence to everyone in that situation, so that you have a very real feeling of what's going on. It's not just abstract; it's your own suffering. It's the suffering of people you know very intimately. But it's also not stuck in that. There's a much more open, wider, huger vision of what the whole thing is about, of what the practice is about, that leads to the development of compassion, the continual opening of the heart. That's kind of the flip side of fear, which is contraction. The other side of fear is an expansion of the mind, which is, again, beginningless, endless, completely open, luminous, empty, wonderful, awesome, ordinary mind.

Emotionality is much closer to my surface now. I am moved to tears much more easily because I think if you really take in what it's all about, it opens up your heart, it opens up your compassion for other people.

I remember very soon after I got my diagnosis when I didn't know whether the radiation to the brain, which is actually the most dangerous thing, was really working or not. I was on my way to a bunch of doctors to get second opinions, and on the way I passed a man who was standing on the street. He had a sign that read, "Vietnam vet with AIDS. Please help."

And somehow as I passed, I looked right into his eyes. Even though I was in a car and he was on the street corner, it was one of those things where our eyes kind of locked, and because of the way the traffic was going I just kept going. I felt so much empathy with him. With the suffering of everybody in this world, he was one particular moving, touching instance of it, and I went around the block and stopped the car.

He had seen me, and then he saw me drive on, and then when I came back he recognized me. I got out and I gave him $20 or something like that. And he just embraced me and said, "Thank you brother." It was very powerful.

At this stage it seems that my disease is something that I have to approach in a different way; it is something I have to be able to live with.

The doctor started talking about managing the disease. My first actions were very aggressive, and, considering the stage of my disease at that time, that was appropriate. But when it came back to a lesser extent and in a more limited area and wasn't immediately threatening my life, then it seemed that the way to approach it was with some kind of accommodation. In other words, to manage it, to keep it down.

Although I am still taking lots of anti-cancer things, they are more of the complementary, Chinese kind, rather than the toxins of chemotherapy. Instead of trying to destroy the tumors, I find myself in a different phase where I have to learn to live with cancer and somewhat coexist with it. I have also added spiritual practices that emphasize more the purification and strengthening of my own body and my own cells. It is more like imagining transformations of the cancer cells into healthy cells rather than obliterating them.

People argue about whether you should be aggressive or healing in your visualization, and I think that, at different times, different strategies are appropriate. It's not one kind of thing. It's more like, I'm in an ongoing relationship with this disease now. Maybe something will come up which will be a cure, but until then the strategy is to figure out how to coexist with this and how to keep it down to a level where it's not life-threatening.

The other day I had a thought that I don't have a life-threatening disease, I live a disease-threatening life. My life is threatening my disease, rather than my disease threatening my life. Threatening in the sense of keeping it from taking over. This is how I feel now.

THE POWER OF LOVE: FAMILY AND FRIENDS

INTRODUCTION

SCIENTIFIC RESEARCH is finally helping us define the role psycho-logical and social support can play in the treatment of illness. There is evidence that social connection—having people to call on for help—reduces the risk of dying from all causes. Our health suffers if we lack social contact. Yet isolation often becomes a reality for people when they are ill. Even well-meaning family and friends may withdraw.

We used to think the fear of dying was really fear of suffering and pain. But a 1996 study in the *Journal of the American Medical Association* found that critically ill patients with AIDS or cancer considered the fear of death, pain, and suffering to be less important than the fear of losing control over how they live and of their bodily functions. They feared losing their dignity and their independence and becoming a burden on friends and family.

But it also is clear, as the stories in this section illustrate, that many times it is *because* of their love for their friends and family that people persevere in the face of a grave illness or a life-threatening situation.

CHAPTER 10

A Cup of Breath

Ellie Bine

I USUALLY HATE CLICHÉS, but there is one I like: "Forget what you did yesterday. Instead, think of what you can do tomorrow." That's what you have to do with an illness like mine—put yesterday behind you and think about what you can do tomorrow to make yourself or someone else happy.

My disease, which is partially a medical mystery, began when I was thirty-nine years old and my children were six and eleven. The doctors decided I have a type of collagen disease. It isn't lupus and isn't quite scleroderma, although I do have some symptoms of scleroderma. Whatever my disease is, it has caused many medical problems over the years, from fluid retention to calcium deposits in my arms and legs.

With some diseases, such as arthritis, people feel better physically when they get up and do things. I feel worse physically but better mentally when I get up, so I decided years ago that I would rather have a happy head than a happy body.

I've found that you can learn to live with not feeling good, once you get over the impatience involved in learning to deal with a disease or a handicap. It isn't something that comes overnight or even in a week or a month. You just have to keep at it all the time. And, once you've conquered it, it's simply a matter of constantly reminding yourself that you can do it.

In spite of being bedridden, I knew I wanted to raise my own children. Someone else could have done it, but I really wanted to, and I pushed myself because it was important to me. Even so, many times I'd do things not knowing if I was going to make it.

I still push myself to do things even when the doctors tell me to take it easy. Although I may just have been lucky, I think my stubbornness is one of the reasons I've survived.

Another reason is my attitude. Attitude can make a physical illness easier or harder to live with.

It's a terrible thing if the first thought that occurs to you when something threatening happens is, "I'm going to die." I have news for you: it isn't that easy to die. Most people who get sick, get well. Most people who go to hospitals leave again and are perfectly all right. The chance of something fatal happening in surgery is less than your chances of dying when you walk out of the house to the bus stop and go downtown.

One of the most important things we all can do is to decide what dying means to us. All it means to me is that I would have to leave the things and people I love. I've always known that the quality of the years you live is far more important than the quantity.

My attitude comes from my mother, a marvelous woman. She was orphaned at the age of five, and by the age of eleven she was cooking for ranch hands and fighting them off. She never had a single luxury until her later years but, in her view, she had everything. Other people mattered more to her than she did to herself. She loved doing things for her husband, children, and friends. She was a woman who could have been as bitter about life as anyone, but she wasn't—she loved life, every bit of it. And you can't live with a woman like that and not get an awful lot out of it.

There were three of us, and we were never allowed to feel sorry for ourselves. Our mother told us, "If you lose an arm, a leg, or both legs—if you can still hear or you can still see or you can still talk—be grateful and make the best of it. You make your own happiness. Don't sit around waiting for everybody else to make you happy."

Another person I take strength from is a young woman named Barbara who was in nurse's training with me. She married, had two children, and, at the age of twenty-six, became paralyzed from polio. When she asked her doctor how long she would live, he said, "Five years."

She lasted seven years and ran her house from her iron lung. She oversaw the cooking, the dressing of her children, everything. So if I indulge in self-pity, it doesn't last long. I just think of Barbara and the way she handled herself. I can still put my arms around my husband and children. Can you imagine never being able to hug anyone? I may not be able to walk well, but at least I can walk straight. I can drive a car, and I can laugh.

I have a friend whose daughter was blinded by someone putting lye in her eye drops. Thirty-two years old. Blind. Yet she has not let it change her life. She goes rowing twice a week with a companion and has a full-time job with Guide Dogs for the Blind. The only thing she hasn't been able to do is fly an airplane.

In the summertime, I often invite children from the *Center for Attitudinal Healing** to swim at my house. The first time they came, I didn't think I could bear to look at ten or fifteen children who had life-threatening diseases. But as I sat in the house, I heard them laughing and splashing in the pool and just having a wonderful time. I went out to watch them play. You would have thought there wasn't a thing in the world wrong with them.

I remember one boy, only nine years old, who had lost both legs and both arms yet always had a playful attitude and always talked about how much he wanted a bicycle. Some students at a college in Florida heard about him and designed a bike with a little seat and a strap that went around his torso so all he had to do to make the bike move was lean forward. The first time he got on and made it go, he was so happy. He just laughed and laughed and had a great time. When I saw him—with no arms and legs—having so much fun and enjoying himself so much, it made me wonder again what on earth I've got to complain about.

If somebody said to me, "Tomorrow we are going to cure you, but the price will be that your husband and children will have great unhappiness for the rest of their lives," I'd tell them to go to hell. When my husband and children are happy, I am happy. If I had to stay in bed

---

*The Center For Attitudinal Healing in Tiburon, California, is an organization for psychological help and healing.

for the rest of my life to ensure that they would never have an unhappy or unhealthy moment, I'd do it. I'm sorry for people who don't have that kind of love to share with a partner and children. It is mainly because of my husband, Rene, that I have managed to cope with my difficulties and stay happy.

When our children were young, they not only had to cope with my inability to go places with them, but Rene, as a doctor, was often called out on emergencies and was therefore unable to be with them. On several wedding anniversaries and birthdays for myself or the children, Rene ended up at the hospital or visiting a patient at home. The children and I learned early that every day had to be an important day. Every day had to be the equivalent of a birthday or an anniversary. Every day was mother's day, father's day, and children's day, even if it was only a part of the day.

We all need to feel useful. How sad that some people feel that to be useful they have to do something spectacular or nearly spectacular. A smile to a tired husband, a reassuring squeeze to an unhappy child, these are little things but so very important.

Since I also need to feel useful, I acted as the message center and key keeper for our neighborhood or as an emergency service for mothers with problems. I couldn't always go to the scene of the problem, but, if I couldn't, I would find someone who could.

I am almost always at home, and, although I enjoy having a beautiful house, what I can see out of my bedroom window is more important to me: the trees. For years people told me to have them pruned, but I wanted them to grow tall so I could see them waving in the wind and hear them batting against the house. Now the branches wander back and forth, flocks of birds come to eat the berries, and the foghorns blow.

Aside from my bedroom, I spend most of my time in the kitchen. I like to cook for people, and the way I handle guests is simply to cook ahead of time and freeze the dishes. For years I had a stool I rolled around on so I could cook sitting down. When it wasn't that bad, I stood up until I couldn't stand anymore. If the stool wasn't nearby, I sat or lay on the floor until I felt better.

I also love going to restaurants, although I am on an extremely low-sodium diet. I've gone into the most elegant restaurants with some salt-free margarine and my own little frying pan in a fancy bag. A doctor's wife once asked me if I wasn't embarrassed to do that, and I said, "No way. I like to eat and I enjoy food. If this is the only way I can do it, why should I be embarrassed?"

A lot of people think that because they're sick, they are different or oddballs. I never felt that way.

I have worried about how Rene felt because I know his concern is very deep, and he doesn't always tell me what he is thinking. One day when I was feeling lousy and couldn't stand up, he phoned and said, "I wish there was something I could do for you." The rest of the afternoon was shot for me. All I could think of was that he was hurt because of me, and that upset me.

It's good when other people care about you, but there's such a thing as caring too much. For me, it has been very necessary to be treated like a "normal" person.

Of course, the other side of that is that I have had to let people know how I want to be treated. People react to you according to how you conduct yourself. I remember once climbing a flight of stairs at a friend's house and having difficulty breathing. My friend said, "Is there anything I can do for you?"

I replied, "No."

And then, in a very light-hearted tone, she asked, "How about a cup of breath?"

People have been exceptionally good to me in my life, yet they haven't smothered me. If they try to, it's good-bye. I need others to accept the fact that I am what I am and am going to do things my way. I've been very selective about my friends because I can't be bothered thinking about what I'm going to say or how I'm going to say it.

I've always been outspoken with my children as well. They don't have to guess what I'm thinking, although I don't tell them every time I'm not feeling well. That's something I need to cope with, not them.

I feel very strongly that people should rely on other people. Support from an empathetic doctor is invaluable, but that alone isn't enough. If the doctor spent twenty-four hours a day with his patients, there is no way he could keep them going. Nor could a husband or a wife. For an ill person, it is dreadfully important to have someone to help you, someone to lean on, just as healthy people do. It's like swimming: sometimes you need to hang on to somebody to get your head above the water and occasionally stretch out your arm and take a rest. But then you have to start swimming by yourself again.

I've been thinking about what motivates people to go on and continue to struggle when they are on dialysis or in a position such as mine. There are lots of tangible reasons—family, the beauty of nature, a nice meal—but there is an intangible one that's hard to define.

It's an intensity that has sustained me and still sustains me even after more than thirty years. I'm in my seventies now. I've lost a finger and a leg and now they tell me I've got lung cancer. But that intensity is still there. I don't know where it came from. You can't tell somebody how to have it any more than you can tell somebody how to love.

Of course, people also need a tangible reason to continue to struggle. And if they don't have one, they had better find one, even if it's the refusal to be victimized by their misfortune. My main motivation was my husband and children, but I probably would have coped anyway because I don't like being unhappy, and I'm basically strong. I like a challenge. I think anyone who sets their mind to it can do anything if they try hard enough.

I have no fear of dying. There isn't anybody who can tell you what comes after death. But it doesn't really make much of a difference. We live our lives every day not knowing what tomorrow holds. I take what comes as it comes. I tell people, "If it would help to worry and worry and worry, then stay awake twenty-four hours a day and worry. But it doesn't help." It must be a terrible thing to be afraid all the time. My philosophy is to quit worrying about things you can't change.

One time I woke up in the middle of the night and said to my husband, "Have you ever thought about dying?"

He said, "Yeah."

"What did you decide?" I asked.

"I decided there was nothing to decide, so I didn't bother thinking about it anymore."

CHAPTER 11

One in a Million

Connie Teevan

I HAD ALWAYS THOUGHT OF MYSELF as a healthy person. I was forty-four years old when I was diagnosed with breast cancer. They found five lumps on a Friday; I was biopsied on Monday and had a mastectomy the following Friday. I knew it was serious, because they were really pushing me along. I knew a little bit about breast cancer. I had fourteen positive lymph nodes, which is not good. I was not very old, and I was shocked about how serious my illness was. My surgeon told me that I needed to start living each day as if it were my last.

This hit me like a ton of bricks. I had a six-year-old daughter, an eleven-year-old son, and a fourteen-year-old daughter who was just starting high school. You do everything you can to protect your children. You send them to the best schools. You send them to special class-es. But I couldn't protect them from the loss of their mother. That hit me really hard, and I started to prepare to die.

I went through all my high school and college things and put together a time capsule, packets of letters and pictures of me for the kids, so they would know me from the beginning, as a child all the way up. You really don't get to know your mother as a person until you're older, and I thought, "They're not going to get to know who I am." I realized that my six-year-old would barely remember me.

I asked my husband, Jim, to start videotaping me. Before, whenev-er he would take videos of us, I'd say, "Oh, turn that thing off, and stop taking so many pictures." Then I thought, "Oh, God, the kids are going to remember me this way." So I asked him to take videos of me smiling and being really sweet.

I also got the family into counseling immediately because I want-ed to get Jim ready to be the mother. I was hoping he could learn to listen better and take on a dual parental role, which is not easy for anybody. Family counseling was very important for all of us because we could talk about scary things during our counseling sessions and then leave those thoughts there, go out for ice cream, and get on with our lives.

Meanwhile, I was trying to wrap up everything as quickly as I could. I'm a very organized person, and I wanted to leave my family in good shape to go on without me. Then, all of a sudden, I knew that I couldn't leave these children. I realized that the best thing I could do for my family was to make a commitment to live.

I immediately flipped to the opposite approach. Instead of prepar-ing to die, I prepared to stay here with my family. I came to believe that if I had a one-in-a-million chance, I was going to be that one in a million.

Several things helped me make that decision. We were all working hard in family therapy, and I saw how important I was to my kids and how much they didn't want to lose me. Also, my doctor had told me about bone-marrow transplants—a very aggressive, state-of-the-art treatment—and that gave me hope that I could get rid of the cancer.

There wasn't any reason not to have hope. It never even crossed Jim's mind that I was going to die. He is a very optimistic person and was always sure I was going to make it. I had the best doctors in San Francisco and they cared about me. I had very supportive friends. Everyone was rallying behind me. So I just started thinking, "I need to be here." Everybody wanted me to live, and there was no reason not to.

I wasn't always positive. When I was in the hospital during my bone-marrow transplant, I had many problems: my kidneys failed, I had severe infections, and I was on many antibiotics. I was in such bad shape most of the time that it was hard for me to have much control or will or ability to do anything to heal myself. Never in my life had I felt like such a passive victim, just lying there at everybody's mercy.

That was a terrifying situation. I had all kinds of hallucinations. I couldn't do anything by myself, and if the nurses didn't have the right IV bags going into me, I was going to die. The Gulf War was going on, but I couldn't concentrate enough to watch TV. I thought they were going to come bomb me. I thought that there'd be an earthquake and everybody would leave the hospital while I was still hooked up to my IV bags. It was probably the low point of my life. I was so dependent and scared.

Many times during my treatment, I felt down, but everybody

around me was giving me the same message: I was going to make it. The partners at my law firm made me a partner when I was undergoing the bone-marrow transplant. Not many law firms would do that. That was a life-affirming act. They believed I was going to come back to work. I was going to be whole.

My doctor had a wonderful woman in his office named Dorothy Mihalyfi who did "New Age" therapy with me right from the beginning. She had interesting ways of looking at things. We often meditated, which is probably conventional now, but at the time it was all new to me. We traveled inside ourselves and cleansed ourselves. We worked on positive thinking and did "hands-on healing" if there was something about our bodies that concerned us.

I joined a support group that Dorothy was leading. I had gone to a lot of support groups where people had what seemed to me to be less serious problems—they'd had lumpectomies and were concerned about what people thought about their breasts—and I had thought, "This isn't for me. I want to be with people who are dealing with life-and-death issues." So I joined Dorothy's group of people with very serious illnesses. Almost all of the group members had been given death sentences.

We did a lot of adventuresome things. We put special objects— things that were important to us—in a basket, and then we chanted to empower them. You might put a healing crystal into the basket. If you were having an important client call, you might put your file in there. I put in pictures of my children. One night we went to the beach, built a bonfire, and danced around it. We shared the different things we were trying. Some of us were doing Tai Chi, some were doing acupuncture, some were on macrobiotic diets.

When I was first diagnosed, my family had been planning a back-packing trip to New Mexico that we had to cancel. When I recovered, we decided to go to New Mexico after all. On the drive through New Mexico with the kids, we stopped at a tiny healing church and gathered the healing sand. When we got back home, my daughter put together a little bowl with the sand, and we put in some of the Native American fetishes we had bought.

It wasn't that the fetishes or the sand or the objects in the basket or any of these had any meaning in and of themselves—I'm a lawyer and I don't take much on faith—but they were all ways for me to live, to be positive, to be life-affirming. They were all ways of enabling me to take control of things. The best doctors were giving me the most aggressive treatment they could, but that's what they were doing. The only way I could take control of my life was to work on healing myself in these other ways.

How would I define the will to live? It's just a conscious decision that you're going to live, and you make sure that everything you do all day, every day, leads to that outcome. You decide that you are not going to die from this disease now, and you're not going to accept anything that tells you differently. You just gear yourself up and that's it.

It wasn't the fear of death that drove me. It wasn't even concern about my husband so much. It was that I didn't want to leave my children. My goals are different now, because my children are growing up. It's a much more selfish kind of thing. Now I want to retire with my husband. I want to travel with him.

I didn't think I was going to live forever, but I needed to make a window of time in which I was going to get my older daughter in college, and my son out of junior high school. Now my aim is to get my younger daughter through high school, and I think I might make it to a ripe, old age. My goals keep expanding. In fact, when I meditate, I envision myself as an old, old, lady. That is such a beautiful symbol to me. I am old and fat and wrinkled, and it is joyful to see myself that way.

Sometimes I feel like a sham because I have been very lucky. I don't know why I'm still here or how long I'm going to be here. Everybody really has to make their own decisions about that. But the most important thing to me is to cut out all the things that tell you that you are not going to make it or that you're at high risk. There are lots of things that intrude and give you the message you are going to die. You have to be very careful. You have to ferret out all the negative messages, even if people think they're not being negative.

For a while, when I'd see my doctors they'd say, "Oh, here's the miracle girl. Look at her. She's doing so well." It sounds like a compliment, but it's not, because it implies that you should have died. When I heard that I would think, "I'm not a miracle girl. Don't talk about this as if it's something extraordinary. This is not unusual. This is just my life. I'm going to live. I'm going to make it."

It's not that I don't get scared or discouraged. It's not that I don't cry or don't ever think I am going to die, but I don't stray from my course.

You have to be vigilant. I loved my support group, but when most of the group that was my age or younger died, I had to leave the group because the message was, "You're next." I never listen to any statistics. I never want to hear them. Never, ever, ever. I purposely block all that out because I don't want to incorporate that negative information. The worst thing that happened to me was reading the letter my bone-marrow doctor had written to the insurance company to get insurance coverage for the transplant. I was very upset to read how serious my condition was. Now I never read or listen to anything that has to do with statistics. There was an article in *Time* magazine about breast cancer. As soon as I came to the statistics, I put the article away. I want to make my own destiny. And my destiny is to live.

The funny thing is, people think you'll change your life completely after an experience like this. You'll quit your job, you'll do different things, you'll live a new life or whatever. But what this experience did for me was to show me how much I liked my life. I used to think, "I should be doing more than this. I should be a more successful lawyer or accomplish more each day. I ought to keep a clean house or study more." I always had these "shoulds" and "oughts." I was always pushing myself, never being satisfied with where I was.

The experience made me see that I was really happy with what I had. I loved everything about my family, my friends, my work, my garden, my house. I just wanted to stay around to enjoy it all. It made me appreciate the normal, everyday things. I'm much more content now with who I am and what I'm doing. I just had to change the way I viewed my life. If I could do anything, I would choose to do exactly what I'm doing now.

I think everyone has to find what's best for them. Really working on staying positive and focused is what helped me the most, and all the other things I did were a means to that end. Maybe I'll need those other things again, but I don't need them right now. But, continuing to maintain a positive attitude is very important for me. Even if it doesn't work in healing me, it still improves the quality of my life, so it's a win-win situation.

CHAPTER 12

A Buddy and a Group

Jack D. Gordon, M.D.

WHEN WORLD WAR II broke out, I was a physician in a station hospital in the Philippine Islands. I had been called up from the reserves to active duty some six months earlier.

When hostilities began on Luzon island, it was apparent we would soon be overrun. We retreated to the Bataan peninsula and reorganized our unit as an evacuation hospital called General Hospital Number 1. What followed was four months of heavy fighting with many casualties. We were directly bombed several times, with five-hundred-pound bombs landing within a hundred feet, making craters thirty feet across. Occasionally, a boulder weighing several tons landed within a few feet of our shelter. As the casualties mounted, we slowly ran out of ammunition and food.

Surrender was inevitable. It came when a line of Japanese tanks passed our hospital on April 8, 1942. The commanding Japanese officer greeted us and officially took us prisoner. Because of this, our surrender was relatively subdued. It was a matter of pure luck. Most surrender activities were quite awful with brutalities, beatings, and even beheadings. What happened to us illustrates a key aspect of survival in wartime circumstances: Luck.

My hospital group was composed of extremely capable and energetic men, well acquainted with each other and with extreme loyalty to the group. Having that sort of support is another key to survival.

Dr. Willie Perilman and I became buddies. And that is another key: It is absolutely necessary to have a best friend to help you survive.

When the Bataan peninsula surrendered and with the defenses at Corregidor still intact, we did not join the march which later became known as "the Death March." Instead, we stayed to take care of the patients in our hospital who could not be moved.

An artillery duel between Corregidor and the Japanese was fought on our peninsula. There were cannons all around us. The shells whistled back and forth almost continuously for a month. Some landed near us, but there were no casualties. Again, a matter of luck.

When we were moved to a prison camp, we encountered a horrible sight. The men were thin and lethargic. The death toll was somewhere between thirty to forty every day. This was down from three to four hundred daily we saw in the weeks before we came to the camp.

Food was scant. It consisted of rice with much dirt in it, some crude greens called *cancon*—which gave everyone who tried it diarrhea, so most of us refused to eat it—some coconut oil, occasionally salted fish, and, rarely, a bit of meat in a stew.

With this diet, deficiency diseases began to appear. I saw several hundred cases of scurvy. Night blindness was common. Beriberi was frequent, causing swollen and later severely painful feet as the swelling receded.

To survive, we had to be extremely careful. A raw vegetable could never be eaten unless it was dipped in boiling water. Mosquito nets were carefully affixed at sundown. We did everything possible to avoid getting diarrhea because of the debilitation which followed. Getting strong and regaining weight was very difficult under these circumstances.

In spite of all our precautions, 1,500 Americans and many thousands of Filipinos perished. Their deaths were ascribed to malaria and dysentery, but the real reason was malnutrition. One does not die from *vivax malaria*. I have often wondered what might have happened if we had just a little bit more protein. In a lush, tropical area surrounded by oceans, fish should have been easily available. Lack of food in those circumstances is inexcusable. Thousands of lives could have been saved with a minimum of such foods added to our diet.

In the camp, it was absolutely necessary to keep the mind occupied with something to which full concentration could be given. A bridge game or chess game, if available, was invaluable. We organized classes. Many men had special training in specific diseases. Dr. Barshop from Los Angeles, where he had been an instructor in a medical school, gave lectures on shock. We organized special classes in linguistics taught by Father Talbot. He was known as "two-gun" Talbot, a brilliant Jesuit who gave lectures in comparative linguistics, beginning with Latin and translating into French, Italian, Rumanian, Portuguese, even Romanish, a dialect in an area of Switzerland. We organized short-story-writing contests. A quartet was formed that sang very credibly. Some Filipino soldiers from the north of the islands made musical instruments. We called them the Cagayan Caballeros.

We read anything we could get our hands on. A dictionary was a treasure. The back of the dictionary contained so many interesting facts. Long novels such as *Anthony Adverse*, by Hervey Allen, were very valuable.

We used to have long talks with each other so that we soon knew the details of each others' families: how many brothers Willie Perilman had, the town where Dan Golenternek came from in Texas, and so on.

Curiously, the sick men in the hospital used to discuss food. They would take turns roster-fashion, "Joe talks about lunch today, Bill has dinner tonight, and Sam has breakfast tomorrow." The conversation would include the name of the restaurant, where it was, what the waitresses were like, how the place settings and the napkins looked, and then the food described in full detail. Some tried to discourage this, but it was no use.

I believe daydreaming is a defense mechanism. If you concentrate deeply while daydreaming, it becomes a time of transcendence. You can't suffer continuously. It's impossible. Nature demands a respite. After a certain amount of time, you must focus on something else, and daydreaming fulfills that need.

Part of keeping the mind and morale positive has to do with studying other people. I was lucky in that way, because I was the attending physician taking care of the officers and corpsmen.

When people became ill and succumbed and you asked, "What happened to so-and-so?" the answer would invariably be, "He gave up." They never said, "He died." It was always, "He gave up." I felt that this was a special phenomenon, probably relating to a kind of a terminal depression. Many of these men had been very ill but were not really sick enough to die. They could have gotten well, but they threw up their hands and gave up their will to live.

I remember a soldier in Bataan, a messenger going back and forth to the front lines. He became ill in the prison camp and was in what we used to call the Zero Ward, or some such name. He was extremely sick. Since our corpsmen had gotten to know him and were fond of him, they offered to help him and get him things, but he refused. He didn't want to eat or even smoke. Just to force some protein into him, I said, "Look, we're going to give you some plasma." He pulled the needle out and died soon after. He had gotten into a mind-set we could not break through.

I was fairly close to this mind-set myself on one occasion. I had mild diarrhea for about three weeks, but seemed to be getting better. One day, I had shaking chills and felt I had malaria. Soon my skin began to get yellow. I lost my appetite. I couldn't take any food for five days, and that's a terrible thing in the tropics. When I realized I had severe jaundice, I felt it was probably amoebic hepatitis and thought my end was near. I really thought I'd had it. I was taken to the Zero Ward.

After a few days, a curious thing happened. First, the diarrhea disappeared and, rather suddenly, I had a feeling of ease. A twinge of appetite returned. I was somehow able to get ahold of a can of beans in tomato sauce. I loved them. Even now, I have a feeling they saved my life. I could eat them without nausea.

As soon as I could stand, I insisted on leaving the hospital, even though the other doctors wanted me to stay. On my way out of the hospital, I stepped on the scale we used for weighing rations. I tipped in at eighty-one pounds. I could barely walk but a step at a time. I would simply run out of strength.

Once back in my cabin, my friends again came to my rescue. Willie Perilman found a can of sardines. Max Andler had charge of the refrigerator where we kept a few medications and concocted something which actually tasted something like ice cream. We had some old C-rations with some cubes of sugar to be used with coffee. Someone gave me several of these, and, when I could walk no longer, I would pop part of a sugar cube into my mouth. And, just like Popeye with his spinach, my strength would suddenly return.

Keeping up our hopes was an all-important factor in surviving this ordeal. Since most of us had not been fully trained, we talked about getting residency training and planning our practice. Thoughts about marriage and family were very helpful.

Other than keeping our minds going in order to stay interested and avoid depression, we had another way of fighting depression: mobilizing anger. Picture a disheveled bunch of dirty guys all lined up and the Japanese camp commander giving them a speech to the tenor of, "You are no good. You're the dregs of the earth. You are my enemies, and our grandchildren will be your enemies, and we don't care if you ever get out of here. Your highest officer begins where our lowest private leaves off."

And in our minds, we thought, "We'll piss on your grave, you son of a bitch."

This had to be a very personal thing. You couldn't say it out loud. You couldn't make a move. So you stood there immobile but inside your anger was boiling. That's the way you had to control it. You learned to stay absolutely deadpan. I have a feeling that mobilizing anger in that way fights depression, and I believe psychiatrists would agree with me.

To summarize my feelings: You need a buddy and you need a group. You have to keep your mind interested and active. You have to exact self-discipline from yourself by avoiding dangerous activities. Finally, you must keep up your will to live. Mobilizing and controlling anger is very important. So is planning for the future and keeping up hope.

While all these factors are important, my survival was, again, mostly good luck. A bomb either hits you or it doesn't. None of the bombs that landed on our hospital struck me, although some were close. I missed the Death March. Staying behind with the hospital group and then going into the prison camp was sheer good fortune. Who knows if I could have survived the hundred-mile march?

On a prison transport on the way to Japan, a ship next to us was blown out of the water by an American submarine. The day before, that ship had been in front of us and not to the side. If the weather had been bad in Hiroshima in August 1945, Kokura, where I was a prisoner, was the secondary target. Nagasaki was a secondary target when it was bombed. Kokura was the primary target that day, but skies were overcast, visibility was poor and the bombers went on to Nagasaki where the sky was clear.

There is the will to live when you are fighting for your life, and there are survival factors that cannot be measured, such as pure, dumb luck.

CHAPTER 13

Still in the Ball Game

Edward Madison

ON MY FIFTIETH BIRTHDAY, I really felt elated. I thought, "Jesus Christ, you've reached a half a hundred years. That's remarkable." I felt I should receive a citation, and I put signs all around the house saying, "Happy Fiftieth Birthday."

I think I was pleased to have reached fifty because I got there without encountering anything I couldn't surmount. Along the way I was besieged by a series of tragedies. I lost my entire family and had numerous disappointments and reverses, so I felt rather good that I had risen to the occasion, that I had been able to keep going. I was scarred, but I wasn't bowed, and I wasn't emotionally crippled.

My friends have taken an attitude of denial toward my lung cancer.

I suppose it's because if they can't bestow longevity on me, they can't bestow it on themselves. They say such things as, "It's got to be a mistaken diagnosis," or, "More than likely you're going to be cured," or, "You can still live to be the oldest person in the world." I've learned to go along with all of these diverse opinions and not to pursue them to the place where it makes my friends uncomfortable.

I have always found my friends to be unselfishly supportive, especially now. Some of them may find it difficult to accept that I have lung cancer because they prefer not to think of me as having such drastic emotional or physical needs. They have always known me to be self-sufficient, leading a somewhat solitary life, even when I was married. Therefore, they have rarely taken my problems seriously.

The decline in my strength and ability has led me to neglect my volunteer activities.

I have written poetry for many years, and I find it interesting to observe how, in different ways, I expressed the same philosophy at eighteen that I do now. I was amazed then as I am now at how human beings, ravaged by circumstances beyond all belief, can mange to stand up despite the unmitigated tragedies that press down upon them. I'm talking about mankind and about people like myself—the survivors and the contributors, people who have become successful human beings.

> Trace the affinity
> Of the will to be
> with the ability
> to be no longer

Ah...such a narrow way divides
And yet, in the precarious clime
of this most eccentric inch
a world of men have lived
Triumphant!

I never thought much about a right way to live. I don't think there is one. And I don't think you always have to look good to be a successful human being. A person can look good on the surface and have as much humanity as a snake. Another person may be a bastard to get along with, but his basic response is full of integrity.

People run the whole gamut—they're nice, they're good, they're bad, they're different. They fail, they falter, they succeed. And they need help. Everyone needs help at some time, regardless of their age or stage of maturity. It's normal, the human condition. It's like saying someone needs love, a meal, or a favor.

It's hard for me to discuss my cancer. I'm not intensely interested in the mechanics of it. All I want to know is the outcome. How long is the cancer going to give me to live, and what is it going to do to my physical and mental abilities? I just want to know my limits so I can work around them.

I know that you can learn to live above and through pain. You may not have the most comfortable life, but you can learn how to harvest those few moments when you aren't in as much pain as you were before. You also learn how to transcend difficulties and how to move across the room, even if it's painful. Pretty soon you can do a great number of things, the pain notwithstanding. Like my knees. I need joint replacements, but I don't know whether I want to be crippled for a month or two from the operation. I don't even know if the replacements would work. My knees hurt a great deal, but I don't notice them as much as I did at first. I just keep moving and creep down the stairs if I have to.

This is not because I'm particularly valiant or strong. That's not my thing. I'm not one of those great heroic personalities. I just think pain is awfully overrated. It's a thing we all fear. But when we eventually face it, we do what we have to do, and we aren't quite as disabled as we thought we would be. Great numbers of people move around every day in tremendous pain.

One thing that concerns me is money. I've held a rather responsible position, but who cares about that? I couldn't afford to quit, because I didn't have any particular skills or formal education. Now I understand I can go on disability and receive forty percent of my salary. I'll probably do that.

I just don't want to end up on the dole. If I'm invited to dinner, I want to be glad to go because of the joy of sharing dinner, not because I wouldn't otherwise have been able to eat. I don't want it to come to that.

Other than the fact that I've lived half a hundred years, time has never impressed me. It's what you do with your life. It's the same with money. It's what kind of mileage you're able to get out of your money or your life. You need money for more than food or rent. Money is needed in order to give presents or to loan a friend five dollars. If you're not able to do that, you won't feel good, so what's the point?

One of my joys of being in the hospital was having time to think. I don't mean I had time to be profound. I wasn't trying to change the world or even change myself. It was just a matter of having the leisure, the luxury, to think anything at all.

It's like what the artist Juan Gris once said to Gertrude Stein, "The little painter has all the things the great painter has. He just isn't great." He's just as meticulous, just as intense a craftsman, tries just as hard, puts as much passion and pain into it. He just isn't a great painter. But all the other externals? He does everything Picasso did—suffers, enjoys, works, is dissatisfied. I'm not a great philosopher, but I have had time to think in my life.

I'm not afraid of dying, but I've been afraid of being a living dead person. What concerns me is the quality of life. A good six months is better than sixteen frightened years. You can pack a hell of a lot of living in six months if you do it right.

The kind of thing I am afraid of is having no interests anymore or losing my mind, becoming a vegetable. Those are the only circumstances under which I might condone suicide—when all the chips are down and nothing can be done and no one is going to be harmed by it. When your life-support machine does not allow you to involve yourself in the business of living, then I think you should pull the plug. You shouldn't have to endure the debasement of never again making a contribution and only being an object of pity.

I think such cases are rare, however. There are few states of disability in which it is impossible to become involved, because as long as you have your mind or even some vestiges of will and speech, you can still be a great listener. You can still be a person who people call, even if you're on a respirator. People can come and unburden themselves to you. There are still contributions you can make.

I've contemplated suicide and even attempted it once, but I couldn't go through with it. One of the things that prevented me was the thought of how dreadful it would be for my friends. It would be a terrible letdown after they had put so much into their friendship and love for me. It seemed like a rotten repayment for the comfort and solace they had given me.

I feel I'm still in the ball game if a friend comes to me with a big problem and upsets me or if he comes to me with a great happiness and makes me feel glad. Either way, it means I have a sincere friend who wants to share a real part of his experience, good or bad, tears or laughter.

I'm looking for the same answers I looked for when I was eighteen. I haven't changed much, but I do know that even with the odds tremendously against you, you can manage somehow to make it.

The vulgar splendor of a noise
Contents the appetite of ears
Insensitive to subtleties.

The really loud occurrence falls
without the benefit of sound
How silently are these:

The awakening of love,
The audacity to dream,
The will to live.

A POSITIVE ATTITUDE

INTRODUCTION

Hope is the most beautiful of all the affections,
and doth much to the prolongation of life,
if it be not too often frustrated,
but entertaineth fancy with an expectation of good.
—Francis Bacon

WE HAVE KNOWN for over 2,000 years—from the writings of Plato and Galen—that there is a direct correlation between the mind, the body, and one's health. "The cure of many diseases is unknown to physicians," Plato concluded, "because they are ignorant of the whole...for the part can never be well unless the whole is well."

Recently there has been a substantial shift in health care toward a recognition of the wisdom of Plato's creed, namely that the psychological and the physical elements of a body are not separate, isolated and unrelated, but are vitally linked elements of a total system. Health is becoming increasingly recognized as a balance of many processes, including physical and environmental factors, emotional and psychological states, nutritional habits and exercise patterns.

Researchers are now experimenting with methods of actively enlisting the mind in the body's combat with disease. To this end, techniques such as meditation, biofeedback, and visualization—the creation in the mind of positive images about what is occurring in the body—are being actively employed in major medical centers along with traditional medicine.

Some people are devastated by the mental and physical effects of illness. Others are able to call upon their inner reserve to sustain them through their crisis, whether it's a short-term or long-term ordeal. Why do some people respond positively to suffering while others are unable to endure?

We have often seen how two patients of similar age with the same diagnosis, degree of illness, and treatment program can experience vastly different results. Why does one not respond well to treatment while the other does? The answer seems to lie in their attitude.

Medical journals consistently report so-called "hopeless" cases where patients have rallied their strength and regained their health. We have witnessed prolonged or unexpected remissions and occasional cures, and we believe that an optimistic instead of a pessimistic attitude was a critical factor.

We are in charge of our actions, but our actions are a reflection of our attitudes. Our attitude can make the difference in how we cope with the challenges we face in our daily life. This, in turn, can affect our level of stress, sense of control over our situation, and our overall health.

CHAPTER 14

To Have Ever Lived at All!

Diane Behar

FROM THE MOMENT I touched what felt like a flat piece of chewing gum almost floating on my right breast, I knew I had cancer. It was November of 1988. I was lying peacefully in bed recuperating from a bad bout of the flu when I unexpectedly came across a strange, foreign presence under my skin which I hoped would simply not be there the next day. But it was. And the day after that. And the day after that.

Terrified to the core, I ran to my gynecologist who, after feeling it for some time, announced that it was probably a cyst, that I was a spring chicken, and that I shouldn't worry about it. Nevertheless, I insisted on having a mammogram and was told that everything was okay. But I never read the radiology report. If I had, I would have discovered that this worrisome new addendum to my breast was "probably benign."

Months passed. The lump did not go away; one day in the shower, I felt it very carefully with my soapy fingers and realized that it had grown. I felt the blood rush out of my face and into my frozen feet.

This time I made an appointment with a breast specialist who examined me briefly and told me, "It's a good thing you came here." When I asked him exactly what he meant by that, he said, "There is a very good chance you have a malignancy."

His words went through me like a hot bee sting. I began crying and couldn't stop. My jaw was bobbing up and down, and I had the sensation of falling through space. He told me to get control of myself as, "We can't have the other people in the waiting room see you like this." Shocked even further by his cold statement, I asked him if he had a back door and ran out of the office.

As though in a dream, I wandered over to the East River and cried and cried and cried into the water. I wanted to crawl out of my skin, which felt like a tight jumpsuit. I knew my life would never be the same.

I eventually found a very warm and caring doctor who put a little pillow under my head while examining me and said, "I would like to see this under a microscope." A week later, he did. While I slowly awakened from my biopsy, he came into my room, stood in front of my bed, and said, "My dear, we have a problem. The lump on your breast was cancerous."

"I know," I said.

He continued. "You will need to have a mastectomy, followed by chemotherapy and probably radiation, and, if you wish, reconstruction. And then you will be fine."

I will never forget those powerful, positive words at the end of his sentence, "And then you will be fine." They almost magically canceled out all the other uncomfortable words that preceded them. They were to be the starting point of my will to live.

For the next year, as I went through the experience of losing my hair, losing my boyfriend, and often my self-esteem, those wonderful words rattled through my brain like a welcome life raft in a turbulent sea. Eventually, they worked their way into the deepest parts of me, even into my bones where I can still feel them today.

In spite of all my ups and downs, I have never doubted the validity of those words. They sustained me through a recurrence of the disease several years later. They have sustained me through metastases to my liver, lymph nodes, and bone. They have sustained me through office visits with doctors and less-than-rosy medical reports. They sustain me more than eight years later as I approach my sixtieth cycle of chemotherapy. I know I will be fine.

This does not mean that I don't have my dark hours. I do. Sometimes often. They visit me like unwelcome guests when I least expect them. They often consume me to the point where I feel so helpless I don't know how I can possibly go on. This is when I turn to the other tools of support which give me strength, courage, and hope.

One of these tools was a welcome guest who visited me when I least expected it. Several years ago, I was taking a bath, feeling very vulnerable and sorry for myself. There is something about the experience of not having hair and sitting like a baby in the bathtub which can bring out some very strong emotions.

At one point, I remember crying so hard that there was nothing left to cry with. Suddenly, I felt a warm, benevolent presence enter the room and fill it with a radiance that startled me. I thought to myself, "So this is what it's like to go crazy." But the presence felt healthy and good, and it stayed with me the rest of the day. I stopped worrying about myself, and, when I smiled, it was a reflection of this calmer, inner state. If I felt the presence begin to drift away, I would close my eyes, quiet my thoughts, and ask it to come back. It always did and would replenish me with a sense of well-being, a feeling that everything would be all right.

Gradually, I began to take a little time each day to become quiet, close my eyes, and focus my thoughts. Over time, I realized that what I was doing was praying, and I would like to believe that the radiance I've come to know is God's love and healing warmth. My close friends tell me that I have a newfound serenity about me. From my point of view, it is my faith in God which is shining through and telling me I will be fine.

I have found that the best time to bring myself into this state of prayer is before I fall asleep at night and after I wake up in the morning. During those times of the day, my mind and body become focused and relaxed. During these prayer periods, I try to let go and release my fears and uncertainties to God and express openly whatever it is that's causing me pain or concern.

Over time, I have found my faith and relationship with God to be the single most important source of my strength and will to carry on.

I get by with a little help from my friends.

—The Beatles

As a single person without a significant other by my side every day, it's easy to feel like a solo dancer. I have been hesitant to enter into a new relationship while I am undergoing treatment. Perhaps it is a way of protecting myself, of conserving all my essential energies for the important task of getting well. But there are times when I see couples strolling together in Central Park or overhear conversations about everyday things like picking up bananas at the grocer when I can feel particularly alone and realize what a boost it is to one's will to live to have one special person to love.

But, for now, my life has been blessed with something else: special people to love.

After I received my diagnosis, I made a promise to myself to eliminate negative individuals from my life and to welcome in those with life-affirming outlooks with whom I could share my precious time. I also evaluated my role in choosing some of those negative people and how my own behavior and patterns may have contributed to negative situations which perhaps adversely affected my health.

I also naturally began to feel close to those people in my life who had positive influences over me and to appreciate my relationships with them that much more. I learned to be more open with them and let them help me whenever I needed assistance, something which was a bit difficult for me as I have always been a very independent person. This experience, in turn, has also given them the opportunity to feel closer to me and be a part of my healing process, for which I am most grateful.

So far, the result of all this effort has been a more relaxed, less stressed-out me who has also enjoyed the adventure of experiencing new faces, places, and possibilities.

The people in my life come from all walks of life and every continent of the world. They are students and professionals, artists and business people, health care providers and homemakers. And when I feel my will to live begin to wane or waiver, I can ring them up or visit them and feel buoyed by their generous spirits.

Because of their presence, I have never felt the need to seek out a cancer support group. My friends and family are my support group, and, although they may never know exactly what I feel, I know they deeply care and are willing to be there for me whenever the need arises. They often tell me that I am so positive, but what they often don't realize is that they are an integral part of this positive outlook. Their words, gestures, and laughter have all gone a long way towards helping me sustain an independent, confident lifestyle as I face the challenges in my life.

One of the most important things I have learned from living with cancer is how to be my own best friend. This has been an essential component of maintaining my health and well-being, both mentally and physically.

The chemotherapy I receive every three weeks usually makes me feel depressed and extremely fatigued and consequently erodes my will to live. There have been days when I have felt too tired to read a newspaper or even make a simple phone call.

One particular tool I developed over time to help me through these rough periods has been a kind of internal cheerleading team that roots me on, picks me up when I am feeling particularly fragile, and gives me the assurance that I will be feeling much better in just a few more days. The team helps to buck me up and get me out of bed when I would otherwise prefer to hide under the covers—even though sometimes I do just that—and encourages me not to give in to myself too much. This internal fan club has enabled me to sustain a more positive outlook during these difficult days.

But the hardest times for me have been when I have received a medical report which contains the words "progression of disease." This happens when the particular chemo I'm taking suddenly ceases to be effective, and I must move on to other drugs. These times are often fraught with a range of very uncomfortable feelings, including fear, anxiety, and despair, and I need to use all the tools in my arsenal to prevent them from overwhelming me.

This is when I call on the group to recite the team cheer: "I have been here before, and I'm back here again, and I'll handle this the way I've handled it before. More than this I cannot do. The rest is in God's hands."

During the difficult times, I also need to pull into myself and seek solitude to rediscover my equilibrium and find what I call "my peace." I often write poetry, which has been a meaningful outlet for achieving this peace. It enables me to frame words, feelings, and thoughts—which at times seem out of control—into a comprehensible structure I can see with my own eyes. This creative process has been extremely therapeutic for me and is something I always recommend to people going through similar crises.

Small Change*

the

fat ladies

count calories

and their

rich men

coins

i

for one

count time

the precious

commodity

of life

marked

in passing hours

measured

and

celebrated

day

by

day

by

---

*Diane Behar, *Collected Poems* (Lunenburg, Vermont: The Stinehour Press, 1998).

day
by
day

carefully
calibrated
and respectfully
recorded
in the book of life
G-ds
private
investment
portfolio

Perhaps the greatest fear anyone experiences who has been diagnosed with a life-threatening disease is that of losing control, feeling cut off from the world, and becoming too dependent on other people. This has certainly been true for me, and, for this reason, it has been very important for me to try to live as "normal" a life as possible.

Of course, when I am in the hospital, I'm not going to an art gallery. When I am very tired or feeling ill, I give myself as much rest as I feel I need. But I also continue to work, travel, and remain as fully assimilated as I can be in the world around me. This world includes both my private, immediate sphere, as well as the outer world of ideas and current affairs. This need to remain involved has enabled me to feel very much a part of the human race and connected to news and events taking place every day. Best of all, it has prevented the illness from taking over my life.

Maintaining a relatively active life, making time for yoga, meditation, and good nutrition, have also been essential "will to live" boosters for me. I have learned a number of visualization techniques I've incorporated into this health regime which have given me a greater feeling of control and mastery over the illness.

When I can integrate a well-balanced routine of all the above, the rewards are evident in terms of having much more energy as well as an overall feeling of calm and well-being. And, when I feel better, the quality of my life is also so much better.

It's a wonderful world.

— Louis Armstrong

My will to live is synonymous with loving life. And perhaps the most precious and useful gifts I have been blessed with have been my curiosity about the world around me and my ability to appreciate beauty. In combination, they have resulted in a lifelong interest in the arts, in travel, and in people beyond my own backyard.

I am absolutely convinced that being surrounded by one's favorite sources of sensory stimulation has as much healing potential as any state-of-the-art therapy. For this reason, I immerse myself in those things which lift my spirits and help me feel larger than myself. I listen to my favorite composers, Mozart and Schubert, and soar with the angels. I visit art museums and thrill at the palette and brush strokes of the great masters. I take a walk in the woods and let the trees and breezes share their secrets with me. Or, I make a special trip to Paris to remember once again how a beautiful city can also feel like a best friend.

The list is endless. I'm fortunate that it is, for I never quite make it to the bottom and must therefore live a long and active life to experience all the wonders there are to enjoy.

One Cold, Winter Evening

It is well past twelve o'clock, and I should be getting into bed, but I can't. I go through this most every night. Trading off precious time for the rest I know I need. But I need this too! This is the very time of day when my mind awakens from a different slumber and enters into a state of enchanted ecstasy that I cherish above most things.

As I sit here quietly, the music of Mozart transports me away on evanescent wings, one aria more transcendent than the next. And here in the safety of my room, I am free to wander across the spectrum of my imagination like a child on an empty beach.

I am truly free! Nothing will do harm to me now. Nothing. Not tonight. Not even the disease which is bargaining for my life.

Here, I am happy just to experience the passage of time. Moment to moment. Feel my breath. Touch my chest. Feel my heartbeat. The perfection of it all! It is so beautiful to behold! And yet, so simple!

This thing we call life is a gift. It is headlines. It enables us limited passage to this precious place we call earth. It is a miracle.

To have ever lived at all! In any century. At any time. Imagine that! To have ever experienced the capacity for feeling and thought and consciousness! To have entered this planet as a human being and not as a weed! To have participated! To have contributed! To have lived!

What more does anyone need to know? Just to appreciate and make the most of whatever is given to us. As best we can. For however long we can. And to give thanks for each and every moment of existence. Even the painful, teaching ones. And to turn one's life over to serving God as His instrument of peace and good.

Yes, Louis, it is a wonderful world.

CHAPTER 15

The Scent of an Orange

Jane Townsend

I THINK ALL OF US are born with a significant will to live that is very powerful. It's not easy to snuff out a life. Death usually comes after many years of living or at the hand of a powerful adversity of some kind. Over time and with experience, each "will" gets individualized and personalized, customized to who we are. We each have a strong willingness to either live or to die.

When I was twenty-four years old, I was diagnosed with Hodgkin's Disease and was treated with radiation therapy. Fifteen years later, I developed another disease, non-Hodgkin's lymphoma, and underwent chemotherapy treatments. That was ten years ago.

At the time, I was depressed and in pain. I felt that I really wasn't getting any better. The doctors couldn't tell me why I was so lethargic and fatigued, and I was getting more and more depressed about it. I just couldn't get my old energy back. Even though my motto at the time was "one day at a time," at one low point I don't think I wanted to live anymore.

Then one day in the lunch room, a friend came in and started to peel an orange. The scent of the orange wafted towards me and, as I smelled it, I felt a thrill, a joyful feeling. I suddenly thought, "I really don't want to die now. I want to smell things like this again." It was in that instant that I began to live with a renewed eagerness, anxious to experience the small joys of life more fully.

This "orange incident" put me back in touch with my will to live. I sat there in pain, smelling the orange, and I was so happy to be alive. I learned in that moment to look beyond the pain to see what else there is in life. I found out then, and since then, that there's always something else. As long as I can find something positive in my life, I'll be okay. I'm pretty good now at finding something joyful just about anywhere, however small it might be.

I'd say that my will to live is based on an "openness" and on a recognition of what I can add to others' lives. I look outside of myself to find more inside. I become bigger and greater if I am an active, positive part of someone else's life.

Staying in touch with my doctors is also essential. I tend to worry, but if I see value in myself and get "good news" occasionally from a doctor's visit, a positive reinforcement takes place, shoring up my reserves. In this way, I can manage my fears more effectively and stay positive in outlook.

We can teach ourselves to do everything we can to recognize and support the notion that we are still alive for some reason or purpose, maybe yet to be discovered, even though we may be suffering. Doing this may seem mechanical at first, but it can work. Soon, we can be joyful in life and cope with the challenges of disease at the same time.

As I've said, openness is my approach. You must be receptive and willing to be open to the truth. This is the key to my resiliency.

Openness is being receptive to all the events of life, even disease. There is a peace of mind that comes when, after being told you have a disease, you realize that only you can control the way you live your life. Openness is the acknowledgment that your future will be different than the one you had dreamed.

I accept what comes my way. I don't complain much. Each complaint takes power from me, power that I need to move forward through doubt, frustration, fear, and pain. Complaining diminishes my will to live and distracts me from my focus on living my life freely and fully.

I seek and dream far beyond the reality of my disease and look to others for friendship, humor, encouragement, and, especially, perspective. Somebody else always has more troubles, more pain. On the other hand, I can always enjoy someone else's pleasures vicariously. I enjoy my personal pleasures, such as growing flowers on my deck, watching children play, listening to music, and reading with eyes that only need glasses. To these enjoyments I add the vicarious joys of Olympic competitors, kids riding skateboards, and expert skiers, human abilities that I as a human can share the happiness and thrill of, even if I am unable to engage in them myself. In a nutshell, I have trained myself to integrate bits and pieces of what is a "blast" in life, in anybody's life.

I am doing well today. Medicine is an evolving and imperfect science. Doctors don't know as much as we would like them to, or as much a they'd like, either. As we care for ourselves, we must be patient patients.

I strive for peace of mind, and I'm enjoying a full life. As a perennial student of my own training, I've discovered that I am far more than simply my body's weaknesses.

CHAPTER 16

Live Life to the Fullest

Sam

Sam's Mother

In the middle of the night of March 2, 1968, a friend of our nine-teen-year-old son Sam phoned to say that Sam had been injured in a skiing accident. He told us Sam's back was broken and that the doctors did not yet know how extensive the damage would be.

A few hours later my husband and I arrived at the medical center and found Sam in traction. The doctors told us that he would be para-lyzed—a quadriplegic—for the rest of his life. I was absolutely crushed. The last time I had seen Sam he had been vibrant, active, and full of life.

My husband told me, "Don't fall apart. Sam has enough pain of his own without seeing more on your face."

All kinds of questions went through my mind. How could this happen to a boy who loves life so much? *Why* did it happen? What can we do for him? Will he regain the use of any of his limbs? Will he be able to sit in a wheelchair? Will he be functional? Can he be a total human being even though he won't be able to walk? The answers would only come slowly, with time, and with hard work on Sam's part.

Sam told us that he wanted to go back to school and be able to drive a car again. He didn't want his hand braces to cause his fingers to be permanently limp. He wanted to be able to eat by himself and didn't want us to have to dress and bathe him. He basically wanted to be independent.

He spent a year in the hospital. His room was always full of his friends, and he also made friends with the orderlies, nurses, and physical therapists. He read and listened to music. He even set up a photography unit in his bathroom where his friends would develop the photographs that he took of them. Centerfolds from *Playboy* were plastered on the ceiling, and posters adorned every wall. A marijuana plant grew in the window. His stereo could be heard at the elevator. Everyone who came to see Sam had a positive attitude.

During his year in the hospital, Sam learned how to use a motorized wheelchair and how to dress himself. It took him quite a few minutes to put on his pants, but he could do it. He could also put on his shirt and button it, comb his hair, and feed himself. His attitude was that there was no hurdle that he couldn't overcome.

Following his stay in the hospital, Sam spent six months in a special training center in Southern California. He was exposed to others with similar problems and was taught to drive again—in a van with a ramp in the back for his wheelchair. Once he was inside the van, he could transfer from his wheelchair to a swivel bucket seat at the wheel where he could operate all the driving controls.

Sam's Occupational Therapist

I worked with Sam very closely. After he realized that he would never walk again and never again have the full use of his hands, he talked with me about death and about living. I could never be anything but honest with him.

I'll never forget the day he showed me some photographs of himself that were taken before his accident. In the photographs he was gorgeous, full of life and fun, standing beside the sports car that he used to race. An overwhelming feeling of sadness came over me. I was overwhelmed by the fact that he was never going to be the way he was in those pictures ever again; he was going to be paralyzed for the rest of his life. I had to make an excuse and leave the room.

When I returned about fifteen minutes later, I told him I had gone to see another patient.

"No, you didn't," he said. "You were crying. I can tell. I can look at myself in the photographs and it's okay. Now you're the one who is realizing that I'm crippled." He could look at himself as he had been and it was all right. It was a pivotal point in his life.

Another turning point occurred at the theater during Sam's first outing from the hospital. He wanted to see the play *Hair* so badly he decided that if the doctor would give him a pass, he would go, and it wouldn't matter who stared at him. He sat in the front row of the theater in his motorized wheelchair in an aisle seat next to his friends.

It just so happened that in the opening of *Hair*, all the actors and actresses would move from the back of the theater toward the stage, holding each other's hands, and stepping on the arms of the theater seats, right over the audience. Sam looked up to see an actor coming toward him in slow motion. As he got closer, he shouted at Sam, "Get your arm off the chair!"

Sam shouted back, "I'm paralyzed!"

The actor said again, "You bastard! Get your arm out of the way!"

Sam shouted once more, "But I'm paralyzed!" Yet somehow he managed to move his arm—just enough—a moment before the actor's foot hit the chair's arm with a thud.

After each performance of *Hair*, the audience would join the actors and actresses on stage. Sam was picked up by some of the actors and carried to the stage to join the others. They gave him drinks, girls sat on his lap, and he got drunk.

The next day he told us that evening was the first time since his accident that he had been looked at as a person and not just as part of a wheelchair. He said the actor who was stepping on the chair arm hadn't cared about him—what had been important to the actor was the show. At the hospital we were all very protective of Sam, but the actor treated him like a normal person, speaking to Sam the way you'd speak to a normal person. That was the first time someone had treated Sam like that since his accident.

A similar incident occurred when the hospital staff taunted Sam into participating in the annual "Wheelchair Olympics" that were being held in Palo Alto, California, that year. He was afraid that he couldn't do it and hadn't planned to attend until the staff challenged him. He did well in the competition, but, more than that, he said it had been a thrill. All of a sudden Sam could swear, get mad, and want to win again. No longer was it, "I'm in a wheelchair." It was, "I'm Sam, and I'm competing against you."

Sam's Mother

Sam returned to college where he became a business major and took a special course to become a computer programmer. There were times when he could not take a class he wanted because it was on the second or third floor. He felt cheated, so he waged a campaign on behalf of himself and others in wheelchairs to have elevators installed in classroom buildings. Quite a few news stories about his efforts appeared in the campus paper. One of them was accompanied by a photograph of Sam in front of a flight of stairs, as though to say, "My wheelchair doesn't have square wheels. Where do I go from here?"

He also campaigned for covered parking areas so that quadriplegic and paraplegics could get out of their cars and into buildings without being drenched in the winter rains. He asked faculty members to give up their parking spaces close to the buildings and asked that space be left between cars so that people could transfer from their cars to their wheelchairs with some dignity. Dignity was important to Sam.

But Sam didn't limit his campaigning to paraplegics and quadriplegics. He went on television to emphasize the plight of all the disabled in San Francisco. He made a plea not only for things like ramps at curbstones but for consideration on the part of bus drivers for the blind, disabled, and aged who can't move fast enough. Sam was instrumental in getting public drinking fountains and telephones lowered to accommodate people in wheelchairs.

When Sam was twenty-three years old, he married Connie, a girl who had been a friend of one of his sisters. Connie had known Sam before and after his accident, so she didn't fall in love with a pitiful young man in a wheelchair. To her, his physical disability didn't matter. She had already fallen in love with him as a person, and she wanted to share all the dreams and aspirations that Sam wanted for himself.

Sam kept his head and accomplished everything he set out to do with the same zest and enthusiasm he had always had, until the second misfortune occurred. Five years after Sam's marriage, almost nine years after his skiing accident, he was diagnosed with a brain tumor.

Sam

The way I found out about my brain tumor is that I kept stuttering and losing my balance. Eventually I found it very difficult to express myself and began to feel like a mental vegetable. The dizzy spells persisted until one day I fell out of my wheelchair. I just didn't know what had come over me and had myself admitted to the hospital. After tests, they discovered I had cancer.

During surgery, the doctors discovered that my tumor was inoperable, but they were able to remove enough of it to relieve the pressure that was causing my speech problems. Over the next several months, however, I lost much of the remaining use of my hands. I could no longer write and had to postpone taking my job as a computer programmer. I underwent radiation therapy, followed by a regimen of chemotherapy.

I went through my greatest depression when I became a quad, but

I also got depressed with the cancer. I didn't lose track of my goals, but the cancer really sabotaged my faith in myself. I didn't know if I was going to be able to drive again or use my right arm again. I didn't know what the cancer meant, and I feared the worst. I felt inadequate and was afraid I would never work again.

After just laying around feeling depressed for a while, I realized how lackadaisical and bored I had become. Boredom—not being able to get out as much as I'd like—was driving me crazy. But the boredom eventually had a reverse effect, making me want to do something constructive.

I began to practice my handwriting again, this time with both hands. I hope to start working part time. There's a limit to what I can do physically, since I'm not as functional as I was before the brain tumor, but I recovered enough mobility to set my goals again. And I want a job I can do by myself, not one that my wife has to help me with. It's more rewarding to do something by yourself, and I want to feel like a full and useful person. It's also important to me to be the breadwinner in the family.

I've learned that there's always one more thing you can do, and you can always do it a little bit better. But, before you can set goals, you have to stop feeling sorry for yourself. Until you do that, you can't re-evaluate your life and decide what to go after. Because of my physical disabilities, things are difficult, but I fight harder because I have someone I love, and I've always had this fighting spirit in me. I want to live life to the fullest.

Sam's Mother

Sam has lived these past ten years with such grace. He has never really become angry or blamed anything or anyone for his problems. He only loses his temper when he attempts to do things he knows he could do but doesn't do them as well as he wants to, because he is a perfectionist.

There is life and there is death. It's what is in between that is important, whether it's a short or long lifetime. If you come into this world and do nothing, you're going to be a nothing. You'll die and no one will know you existed. A lot of people live a long time and might as well not have lived at all. They survive life. Instead, as Sam has taught us, you have to live with great gusto, with everything you've got.

Sam has fully lived his life. He wants his life to be of some value. He knows that he has something to give, and he gives it in the best way that he can. That's why I don't pity him. I'm as grateful as he is that he has lived as long and as well as he has. He has given me more in his 29 years than I could ever give anyone, even if I live to be 150 years old.

CHAPTER 17

In Touch with My Dream

Alan J. Cooper, M.D.

AFTER THE INITIAL SHOCK of learning that I had cancer—malignant melanoma—and worrying through two recurrences, I concluded that the only quest in life that made any sense for me or gave me any sense of purpose was to get "cured."

I asked several oncologists to advise me of ways to conduct my life that might enhance the chances of cure, but I received no worthwhile advice other than, "Stay out of the sun." The medical profession doesn't even know if that advice makes any difference once the cancer had occurred.

I also asked what it meant to "fight," since we have all heard that those who fight survive longer. There were no concrete suggestions in this area either, although most oncologists do believe that a fighting attitude helps somehow. I was left feeling suddenly alone as a "patient" and increasingly distant from the assurances and help of my colleagues.

I decided to explore every aspect of life that might hold promise for effecting a cure. I continued to receive the best available conventional therapy for my illness, but I also took part in experimental therapy.

It seems entirely possible that there are mechanisms within the total neurophysiological structure of a person which bring about a restoration of health by entirely natural means. The triggering factor could be mental, physical, or spiritual. The process might take seconds or years. I didn't see any value in excluding such possibilities.

I realized early on that I would be adopting measures in part based on intuitive or inner validation rather than on any external structure of proof. I have not regretted this approach. Indeed, it has immensely enriched my life.

The first step for me was to take stock of my life in the broadest sense. I was helped very much by the exercises described in Alan Lakein's book, How to Get Control of Your Time and Your Life*.

To my surprise, I found that the most important thing on my list of what I meant to accomplish in life was attaining inner peace. Dr. Jerry Jampolsky at the Center for Attitudinal Healing in Marin County, California, defines "healing" as precisely that: the attainment of peace.

Many other aspects of my life-plan emerged from reading Lakein's book as well, and I highly recommend it to anyone drifting along in life who hasn't discovered their particular purpose or meaning.

---

*New American Library, 1996.

Through this process I have accomplished a number of things I would never have done if I had not had cancer, including running in the San Francisco "Bay to Breakers" race.

I want to make it clear that the value of listing life goals and then doing them is not just to enjoy life "while you still can." That kind of attitude is self-defeating. Rather, the value is that, by becoming active in doing things that are truly and deeply meaningful, I began to restore some physical and emotional balance to my life and actually realized the possibility of a physical cure.

There is a Native American belief that when a man loses his dream, he begins to die. I realized that I had indeed lost touch with my personal "dream." I have tried a smorgasbord of things to help me get back in touch with my dream and to re-establish my positive feelings and energies.

I have practiced both receiving and giving love; I've gotten psychological counseling from a man trained in the thought process and theology of Lawrence LeShan; and I have used sleep time to listen to a wide variety of tapes on health and life. I have overcome inertia and discovered that all kinds of things I hadn't thought I could do are possible.

I've strengthened my ability to have faith. It is hard to believe in the efficacy of external factors (immunotherapy, exercise, etc.) if we don't nurture the impulse of faith itself, especially if our body seems to have failed us. Increasingly, I turn the whole process over to God whenever I can. The feeling of peace and power that comes from the act of letting go and, occasionally, from prayer, seems to ratify that the universe is on my side.

I must have tried all the many varieties of prayer. Some have been quite moving. I have also experimented with the use of affirmations—uplifting positive statements—repeated many, many times, such as, "I am healthy," or, "God loves me."

Visualization has also been very helpful. I have used several forms of visualization, including seeing and feeling myself healthy, successful, and happy in the far distant future in which I love myself. I've used a visualization in which I see myself healed by significant other people, and another very important visualization in which I address all the organs of my body with gratitude and respect for a prolonged, healthy life. Along with visualization, I have used self-hypnosis to more deeply reconstruct my attitudes and self-image.

Bodily, I have found regular vigorous exercise to be important. I run three times a week and "wrestle with rocks in my living creek." I also follow a strict vegetarian diet and take vitamins, including high doses of vitamins C and A.

Since embarking on this program to re-establish my positive feelings and energies over a year ago, I have scarcely had a single moment of depression or hopelessness. Such feelings occasionally start, but I seem to be able to stop them cold. To me this is a minor miracle following three operations and a lung metastasis.

My doctors have always projected a healthy optimism. I can't tell you how uplifting and energizing this is once you have had a life-threatening illness. There is such a large body of negative programming out there that any positive statements, actions, and feelings seem not only justified, on the basis of "equal time," but necessary in order to positively influence our immunity.

There seems to be a kind of subliminal, self-fulfilling prophecy in many of the communications received from people about cancer.

Conventional opinion assumes cancer to be a kind of slow death. Even the kindest of friends look morose as they ask how you are. The powers of the community are such that people can enhance the likelihood of death from cancer simply by projecting such a negative attitude subliminally.

Another important area of negativity appears in statistics about melanomas or any other illness. Such statistics may have no bearing on me. Someone who survives a particular illness for five or ten years may be a one-in-a-hundred or one-in-a-thousand statistic, but, for themselves, they are a hundred-percent survivor. I chose to be such a person, since I enjoy not being a victim. Why not be a victor?

The process of separating myself from the conventional wisdom that all cancer ends in death is just beginning, and I have only partially rid myself of self-defeating attitudes. I have learned not to call myself a cancer patient because I have not stopped being myself just because a melanoma happened to me. I don't intend to change my identity at this time because of a disease.

Although it might appear that I'm only concerned with "positive" things, I am increasingly aware of the destructive forces within me, especially Fear, with a capital "F." Part of my program involves facing fears one by one, getting to know them, and then doing something about them.

Action is one of the best antidotes for fear. A lifelong fear of mine has been of standing in front of a group of people and leading them or lecturing to them. I therefore started giving classes during the past few years about deep relaxation and imagery techniques that lead to changes of attitude as well as to some physiological changes. Doing this has given me a great deal of confidence, and I plan more classes, possibly for cancer patients.

More than once I have caught myself imagining how I would have to die in order to be memorable. But there is no profit conforming to others' expectations that cancer patients must die bravely, heroically, philosophically, spiritually, or any other way. People with cancer needn't be scapegoats for other peoples' fear of death.

I'll never forget the words my oncologist recently spoke to me. They have been ringing in my ears, mind, and heart ever since. He reviewed my records, looked up with surprise on his face, and said, "Why, Alan, your body seems to have done an amazing job of controlling your cancer. I think you may well be cured." He has made similar remarks on all subsequent normal examinations.

In closing, I must say that illness for me has been a gift and a springboard into new life. I've been able to resurrect hope and fun and to rediscover the value of leisure and laughter. I suspect all those legendary, 120-year-old men sitting around in the Urals sipping their vodka are also telling and retelling 100-year-old jokes that we ought to go listen to.

CHAPTER 18

Recharging My Batteries

Joanna

IN JUNE OF 1985, I was diagnosed with breast cancer. I had surgery, including reconstructive surgery, chemotherapy, and a short tamoxifen treatment. At that point, I was not worried. I knew the surgery had been done soon enough, and I was convinced that I was cured.

However, in October of 1989, I was diagnosed with a recurrence in the ovaries. When giving me the news, the oncologist told me, "This is incurable." Thank God, I have strong spiritual beliefs. Otherwise, I could have given up right then and there. I firmly believe that God is my creator, and He knows how to heal me. To Him, all things are possible.

Again I received chemotherapy treatments and then hormone treatments, to no avail. I was going from bad to worse. The sterile atmosphere of the doctor's office added to my misery. At one point I was almost suicidal, and I requested a friend to come and live with me.

By the summer of 1991, my abdomen had swollen to the point where I looked like I was ready to give birth. I was in pain. I contacted an acupuncturist to help me with the pain and confided to him that I had had doubts all along about the treatment I was receiving. He reminded me that I should always trust my instincts and prompted me to obtain a second opinion. He asked his other patients for recommendations for an oncologist.

The physician he found for me reacted so fast that, now seven years later when I think about it, my head still spins. The new oncologist referred me to a gynecologic oncology surgeon, and I am sure that these two doctors saved my life. Their words of support before the surgery meant a great deal to me and sustained me through the entire ordeal. After recovering from surgery, I underwent a long course of chemotherapy.

I can't stress enough how important it is to trust and like your doctor. The oncologist I found by way of my acupuncturist has an office with a warm family atmosphere. Everyone there is helpful, friendly, and cheerful. After chemotherapy treatments, his wife always checks with the patients to see how they are doing. I find this very reassuring. I also feel completely free to speak my mind and ask questions, knowing that I will always get a straight and honest answer. At various times when I was very disheartened, the doctor's wife comforted me and took the time to counsel me. All this is invaluable support for someone living alone facing a serious illness.

After eleven surgeries and more chemotherapy here and there, I am currently working full-time for a large law firm in San Francisco. I work long hours, but only three days. It is a great schedule that enables me to receive any treatment I need and still be productive. On my days off, I can watch my food intake, concentrating on eating organic vegetables, fruit, and meat and milk that are free of hormones. I also have time to exercise. I find exercise very relaxing not only for the body but for the mind as well.

I enjoy the company of my coworkers, who are an integral part of my support group. I really feel that being able to continue working has contributed to my coping with the illness.

I live alone, and yet I have a wonderful support group: friends, coworkers, my physician, his wife, and their staff. Faith in God has also helped me a great deal along the way.

Throughout these twelve years of fighting cancer, there has been plenty of depression, and at times a very strong urge to give up, refuse treatment, and just let go. But somehow, at these moments, there always has been a dear one near to remind me that I have a lot to live for—all the people I love, and all the many things there are to still discover, all the places to visit, and all the new skills to acquire.

I have made a "Dreams Envelope" for myself, consisting mostly of lists: people I cherish, countries to travel to, and numerous personal projects. When I feel the urge to stop fighting and give up, I go through my Dreams Envelope lists. It never fails to bring back my will to live. There is still a lot for me to enjoy and discover. It is not time to go yet.

As to how I recharge my batteries when the going gets rough, it is somewhat varied.

I enjoy reading very much. A spiritually oriented book or one of the cancer-survivor stories I have collected over the years always picks me up.

Beauty in the arts is an important healer for me. I have taped a number of ballets, operas, and concerts. I have wonderful books of painting reproductions, and I attend performances and exhibitions as often as I can afford it.

Nature is also a favorite. Walking in the park or on the seashore energizes me. Watching a funny movie with a friend is therapeutic.

Another thing I find very soothing is to enjoy complete silence in my apartment for a whole day—no music, no telephone, no television. Just light food, a lot of water, and reading a favorite book. It's almost like a retreat, and afterwards I always feel renewed and ready to pick up. It is like giving my mind a shower!

In a way, this illness has had a liberating effect on me. It has forced me to reevaluate my priorities. I avoid negative people. I fret less over small annoyances, and I am learning to take care of myself and no longer place the needs of others ahead of my own needs. I am also training myself to enjoy each day thoroughly and be thankful for it.

CHAPTER 19

An Inner Fire

Susan Yoachum

Part One*

I have metastatic breast cancer.

Metastatic is a tough word to spell and an even harder one to say, but its meaning is rather simple.

It means a runaway mine train is careening through my body. Or, in clinical terms, it means my cancer has spread to "vital organs"—a phrase that somehow seems redundant.

---

*From an article by Susan Yoachum in the *San Francisco Chronicle*, September, 14, 1997.

I have known this since April 25, 1997, two weeks before I turned forty-two.

Not much seeped through the numbness at first, but I will tell you that one of my first conscious thoughts was, "No, I can't go yet. I haven't read all the classics."

As if to ward off evil spirits, I've gone out of my way since then not to read the classics, but rather to read an eclectic mix of books on healing as well as utter trash fiction.

When I progressed to even darker humor, my first thought was, "At least I'll never have to learn the Internet." This thought has had a positive effect. My Internet coach says he'll have me Web-browsing in no time.

There are times when I feel like a whiner, self-absorbed and self-obsessed. That feeling peaked again when I got some bad news—my cancer had spread further. When I entered the treatment room I was shaking with tears. With tears in his eyes, the technician I knew from my brain radiation hugged me, and my tears turned to sobs.

I lay, face down, for the treatment. Fifteen minutes later, at the end of the session, the pillowcase was soaked. I felt enormously sorry for myself.

But as I walked out of the treatment room, my friend the technician tapped me on the back and inclined his head toward a gurney. A boy of about twelve was lying there, waiting for his radiation.

I asked, "Will he be OK?"

The technician said he didn't know.

There are worse things than cancer spreading to your bones after all. As the days pass, I'm forging an uneasy peace with this cancer that defies answers.

How many times in therapy-kissed California have we heard that the only things we can control are our own responses to what befalls us? This diagnosis brought me up short again. After having thought for the first few days that my life was ending, I realized that it's not over till it's over—and I began living again.

When I'm able to work, I find it intellectually challenging and the company of my colleagues and comrades comforting. Once again, my family and friends have appeared from everywhere to help share the burden.

Most often, they say that they don't know what to say. That's OK. Neither do I. I never had metastatic breast cancer before.

But I do know that when a friend hugs me close, I feel connected to life.

And in the middle of the night when the demons come, I take out all the cards and notes and phone messages, and for a few hours, I let all my loved ones carry the burden. And when I take it back up in the morning, it's not quite so heavy.

I have a very clear idea of the special quality of each day, and I've been urged repeatedly to take a trip, which I'll probably do after my treatment schedule settles down.

But, once again, I count myself lucky. I get up every day with a husband I love, work that fulfills me, and family and friends who nourish me. Paris, Venice, and the Great Barrier Reef beckon, but this is the good life, here in San Francisco.

Today.

Now.

Part Two

I'm an inhaler. I know this because a dear friend recently told me that I "inhale" life. For me, that's what the will to live is all about.

The will to live is a feeling of not being through yet, of there being things I want to do, people I want to love, places I want to see, and work, in the broadest sense, that I feel I've left undone. Metastatic breast cancer has both strengthened and weakened this God-given gift.

One thing that has strengthened my will to live has been the enormous support that I've gotten from my family and friends. It's made a really big difference to know that they're out there. When I'm feeling really low and thinking, "Oh, I can't do this any more. This is just too hard," then I'll think about what somebody has said in a telephone call or left on a phone message or wrote in a card, and that tremendously strengthens my own will to live.

My husband Mike has been incredible. He's been a rock. He feeds me, he nourishes me in every possible way, and he has been quite remarkable. He really understood what my cancer meant before I did, and that helped me when I had to deal with some very hard truths about what it meant for me and for the rest of my life.

I'm coming to terms more all the time with the fact that I have an incurable illness. It can go into remission, but it's always there; it's chronic. I will always have it, and that's hard to accept.

There were a number of times when I fell asleep at night, and I wondered if I would wake up in the morning. I realize that, at some point in time, that's probably going to be repeated, but this only strengthens my desire to get everything I can get out of each day. I like living.

Even though I'm always aware that I have cancer, I don't always think about the fact that I have cancer, especially when I go out to play in my garden or am having a good time playing Scrabble or reading or doing something else.

The will to live is an inner fire. Sometimes, it burns more brightly than others, but it is always coming from inside you. My will to live, in addition to the support, prayers, and good thoughts of my family and friends, is what keeps me going.

CONCLUSION

The Will to Live

> Look to this day for it is life,
>
> For yesterday is already a dream,
>
> And tomorrow is only a vision.
>
> But today, well lived, makes every yesterday
>
> A dream of happiness and every tomorrow, a vision of hope.
>
> —Sanskrit Proverb

AND SO IT IS with this elusive feeling we call the will to live.

The will to live comes from hope but is nevertheless rooted in stark reality. The people in this book—and thousands like them—know that it is a difficult balancing act to maintain a strong will to live in the face of debilitating treatment, excruciating pain, and sometimes persistent bad news.

But they chose to consider this constant reminder of our fragile mortality as a "wake-up call" that led them to reassess their values and to either confirm or change their way of life. Each of them nurtured old relationships and developed new ones; each lived life more fully while learning to live with illness. Each of them found hope.

The same opportunity to acknowledge our mortality and examine our priorities is available to all of us, the "temporarily healthy as well as the ill," as David Spiegel mentions in his introduction to this book. What is important to us? How do we want to live the rest of our lives? If we discover behaviors or habits we wish to change, we are free to begin experimenting in that direction. We too may start to take risks, open our minds to other modes of thought, take a trip or a class, and make new friends. Anyone who goes through this process will undergo permanent, positive change and will have begun to nurture the will to live.

Although we cannot precisely define the will to live, we have identified the following attitudes and behaviors common to those in this book as well as to other patients observed over many years of practice:

1. They live in the present. They know the past cannot be changed, but they also know they have the capacity to influence the quality of today and tomorrow.

2. They accept their new problems and attempt to solve them through introspection, understanding, and sharing.

3. They set reasonable, achievable goals.

4. They consciously try to downplay negative emotions and to focus on feelings of love and hope.

5. They surround themselves with supportive friends and family members.

6. They actively search for ways to help others.

We, as care givers, consider the first five attitudes and behaviors to be essential. Those who practice them are ensuring that their needs are met. The sixth represents a principle we have long recognized as vital to a fulfilling life: Try every day to help someone else! When our own needs are met, we are emotionally free to give to others. For Ellie Bine, it was giving an unhappy child a hug; for Edward Madison, it was sharing the joys and sorrows of a friend. As a result of their suffering, these people discovered they had something special to give.

Of all the ingredients of the will to live, none is more essential than hope. But hope is relative: One person may hope for the fullest possible remaining life; another may hope to live until a special holiday or a family reunion; still another may simply hope to avoid suffering.

Doctors can contribute substantially to a patient's feelings of hope—not false hope, but realistic hope. When a patient asks, "How long have I got?" some physicians will respond: "six months," or "a year," or "two years," and quote clinical statistics for that person's disease. What these physicians often forget to mention is that statistics are "averages," compiled from survival data on a great number of individuals, some of whom obviously lived much longer than the average, and others a much shorter time. As many of the individuals in this book demonstrate, it is impossible to predict any person's longevity. Even after a patient has begun a particular therapy, it takes time to determine whether it will have the desired effect. But even if it fails, another one may be highly successful.

Hope may indeed be one of the elements that enables a person to live longer than medically anticipated. However, the opposite is also true. An extreme lack of hope can have the same effect as the phenomenon called "self-willed death" or "bone pointing,"* observed among

---

*G. W. Milton, "Self-Willed Death or the Bone-Pointing Syndrome," *Lancet*, June 23, 1973: 1435-37.

Australian Aborigines and in other South Pacific cultures. In such cases, a tribal "witch doctor" casts a spell similar to that observed in Voodoo, causing the victim to suffer paralyzing fear, withdraw from society, and die within a short time. Of course, the witch doctor can only be effective if the potential victim believes in the power of the curse. In the same way, a person with an illness can be adversely affected when doctors and nurses project a sense of hopelessness, or when family and friends are unable to hide their fears. (Paradoxically, such people are often projecting concern over their own mortality, not that of the patient!)

Clearly, hope is a life force in and of itself. A little hope—a remote chance for survival or a small improvement in one's condition—can give the strength to carry on.

There is no medicine like hope
No incentive so great
And no tonic so powerful
As the expectation
Of something better tomorrow.
—Orison Swett Marden

In conclusion, the will to live both defies definition and has many definitions, as demonstrated by our contributors. We can only describe common behaviors and attitudes among those who have it, and acknowledge its wondrous power. People who exhibit a strong will to live appear to have strong bonds of friendship and love. They also show a determination to meet misfortune head on, to accept what has happened, and find a way to cope. Part of this process involves finding out everything they can about their condition and treatment alternatives and discussing these facts with their doctors and those close to them. They certainly reexamine their priorities. Most important, perhaps as a result of the foregoing, people with the will to live are determined to live life to the fullest, be this for one week or a natural life span.

Finally, most of us do not discover the great, untapped force of the will to live until we are faced with an illness or other crisis. Yet we all have the ability to unearth its potential. We hope that the stories of the courageous people in this book will inspire you to delve into your innermost being and live every moment fully from your mind and heart.

Rekindle your Inner Fire,
Your will to live.
You still have time to live.
How you live is your decision.

Also by Ernest H. and Isadora R. Rosenbaum

Living With Cancer
New York, 1975, Praeger Publishers.

Mind and Body
San Francisco, CA, 1977, Life Mind & Body.

Health Through Nutrition
San Francisco, CA, 1978, Alchemy Books

Comprehensive Guide for Cancer Patients
Palo Alto, CA, 1980, Bull Publishing Co.

Decision for Life
Palo Alto, CA, 1980, Bull Publishing Co.

Nutrition for the Cancer Patient
Palo Alto, CA, 1980, Bull Publishing Co.

Rehabilitation for Cancer Patients
Palo Alto, CA, 1980, Bull Publishing Co.

Sexuality and Cancer
Palo Alto CA, 1980, Bull Publishing Co.

The Cancer Patient's Guide to Social Services and Hospital Procedures
Palo Alto, CA, 1980, Bull Publishing Co.

Going Home: A Home Care Guide
Palo Alto, CA, 1982, Bull Publishing Co.

Art For Recovery •
San Francisco, CA, 1989 Mount Zion Medical Center.

Supportive Cancer Care: A Comprehensive Guide for Patients and Their Families
Toronto, Canada 1998, Sommerville House.

Also by Ernest H. Rosenbaum M.D.

Living With Cancer, 2nd Edition
St. Louis, MO, 1982, Mosby Library.

Can You Prevent Cancer?
St. Louis, MO, 1983, C.V. Mosby.

Nutrition for the Chemotherapy Patient
Palo Alto, CA, 1990, Bull Publishing Co.

You Can't Live Forever: You Can Live 10 Years Longer With Better Health
San Francisco, CA, 1993, Better Health Foundation.

Everyone's Guide to Cancer Therapy
Kansas City, 1991, Sommerville House and Andrews & McMeel.
1993 2nd Edition, 1997 3rd Edition

Planning For The Future
San Francisco, CA, 1996, UCSF / Mount Zion Medical Center.

About the Authors

Ernest H. Rosenbaum, M.D.

Clinical Professor of Medicine, University of California, San Francisco; Associate Chief of Medicine, University of California, San Francisco/ Mount Zion Medical Center; Medical Director, Better Health Foundation, San Francisco.

Dr. Rosenbaum's career has included a fellowship at the Blood Research Laboratory of Tufts University School of Medicine (New England Center Hospital) and M.I.T. He teaches at the University of California, San Francisco/Mount Zion Medical Center, and was the cofounder of the Northern California Academy of Clinical Oncology.

His passionate interest in clinical research and extraordinary communication with patients and colleagues has resulted in the publication of more than fifteen popular books on living with cancer and over fifty articles on cancer and hematology in various medical journals. A frequent guest on radio and television programs, he also lectures widely to various medical and public groups.

Isadora R. Rosenabum, M.A.

Isadora Rosenbaum is a medical assistant who has worked in immunology research and an oncology practice offering advice and psychosocial support for patients and their families. She is the coauthor of a dozen popular books on living with cancer and supporting the cancer patient.

For More Information

Visit the *Inner Fire* website at **www.innerfire.com.**

To order additional copies of *Inner Fire* with your credit card, call toll-free 1-888-626-9662.

Or send check or money order for $14.95* + $4.00 shipping and handling to PLEXUS, 815-A Brazos, Suite 445-Y, Austin, TX 78701.

For information about other books and tapes published by PLEXUS, please request a catalog at the above address or call our order line toll-free 1-888-626-9662, or send us email at info@cyberplexus.com.

*Checks must be in U.S. dollars drawn on a U.S. bank.
Texas residents add 7.25% (Austin 8.25%) sales tax.